By Billy Childish*

Back on Red lite rd (1981)
2 Minits Walk from 10 am (1981)
The First Creatcher is Jellosey (1981)
Black Things Hidden in Dust (1982)
You me Blud and Knuckle (1982)
Big Cunt (1982)
Prity Thing (1982)
7 by Childish (1982)
Will the Circle be Unbroken (1983)
10 No Good Poems of Slavery, Buggery, Boredom
    and Disrespect (1983)
Nothing Can Stop this Man (1983)
Poetry Like Dirt (1983)
The Unknown Stuff (1983)
Poems from the Barrier Block (1984)
Tear Life to Pieces (1985)
Poems without Rhyme, without Reason, without
    Spelling, without Words, without Nothing (1985)
Monks Without God (1986)
Companions in a Death Boat (1987)
Conversations with Dr X (1987)
To the Quick (1988)
The Girl in the Tree (1988)
Maverick Verse (1988)
The Silence of Words (1989)
Admission to Strangers (1989)
En Carne Viva (Spanish/English) 1989
Death in a Wood (1989)
The Deathly Flight of Angels (1990)
Childs Death Letter (1990)
Like a God i Love all Things (1991)
The Hart Rises (1992)
Trembling of Life (1993)
Poems of Laughter and Violence (1993)
Hunger at the Moon (1993)
Days with a Hart like a Dog (1994)
Poems to Break the Harts of Impossible Princesses
    (1994)

Translation, with K. De Coninck
(Cannon-Fodder by L.F. Céline (1988)

* B. Childish is dyslexic, these poems appear as
  written by the author.

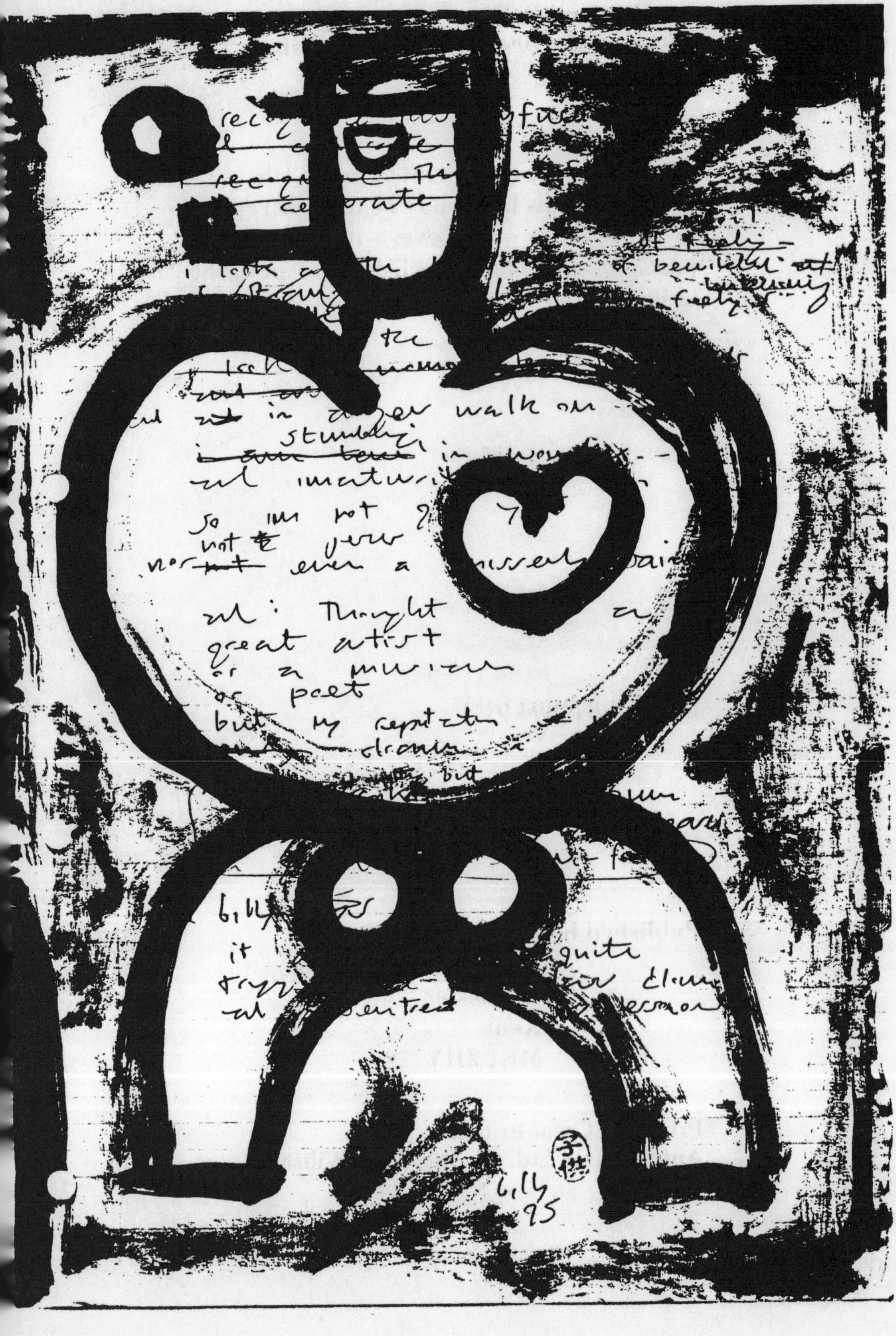
walk on
great artist
or poet
billy
95

ISBN: 1 871894 91 3

Published by Hangman Books
        2 May Road
        Rochester
        Kent
        ME1 2HY

Printed in Great Britain by
Antony Rowe Ltd, Chippenham, Wiltshire

BIG HART AND BALLS

(POEMS AND DRAWINGS)

Billy Childish

HANGMAN BOOKS

this will change

Table of Contents

dead funny

i am a thorn in the side
of the establishment

my success annoys everyone
to the extent that even i pretend
not to be successful

my adolescent concerns
are the bore of the town
my friends hiss at me
and ex-lovers wish me dead

honestly even my own mother
cant bear to read my texts

it seems ive painted a lot of shit
so much so that i meet complete strangers
who presume that i swim in it with glee

and with every poem i rite
my fame grows
another nail in my coffin
people feel embarrassed for me
everything i utter becomes a cliche

when oh when the people ask
will billy shut up?

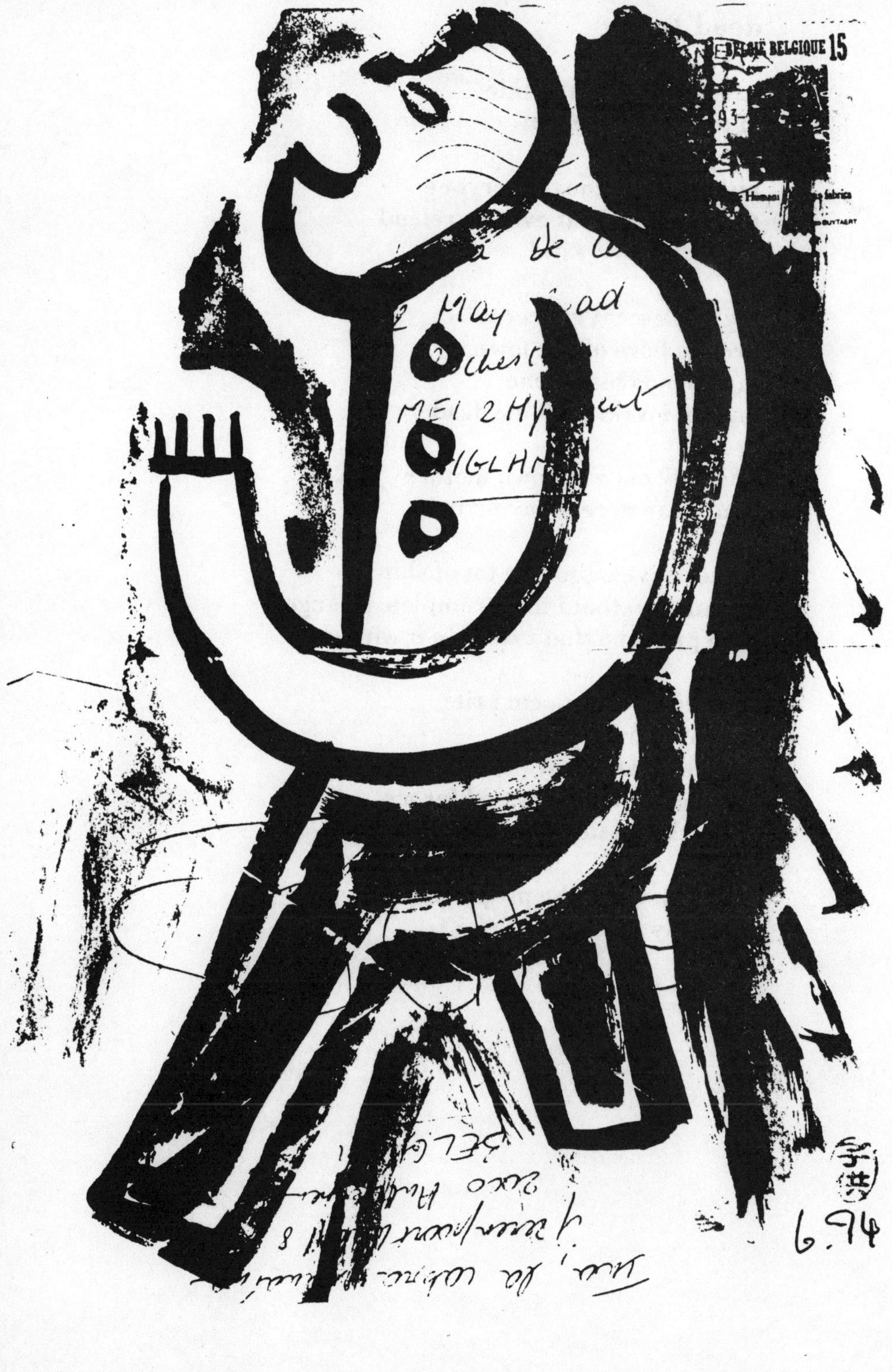
BELGIË BELGIQUE 15
6.94

gods own bastard

each morning i look
to the mirror
and tell myself
that im loved
that i am a divine
manifestation of god

that there is plenty
for me in this world
that i have a beautiful smile
beautiful eyes and lips
and to let go this mind
littered with
the possessions of others
with cravings and wants
i didnt even know i owned
hidden lifetimes of misery
and repetion

asks billy
whose mess is this
but gods own bastard?

MR BILLY CHILDISH
CARE OF / ULI SCHEIBNER,
SCHONEWORTH 18,
3 HANNOVER 1,
GERMANY

FROM :- MS S. LEWIS
16 ORDINANCE STREET,
CHATHAM, KENT,
ENGLAND

IF UN DELIVERED &

billy 94

quivering with expectation

who is this billy childish?
the people ask
this rogue in our midst?

i do not know him
hes a stranger to me also
he tilts his hat and adjusts his dick
like hes god gift

he barges to the head of the queu
claps his hands and announces himself
his lips quivering with expectation

he denies himself all
then pushes himself to ridiculous extremes
hoping to be saved at the precipice
by gods hand and declared a saint

he is full of noise and bravado
but i repeat i do not know him well
we just used to get drunk together
thats all
and hed always get me in deep trouble
but boy could he laugh
and he always smiles so convincingly

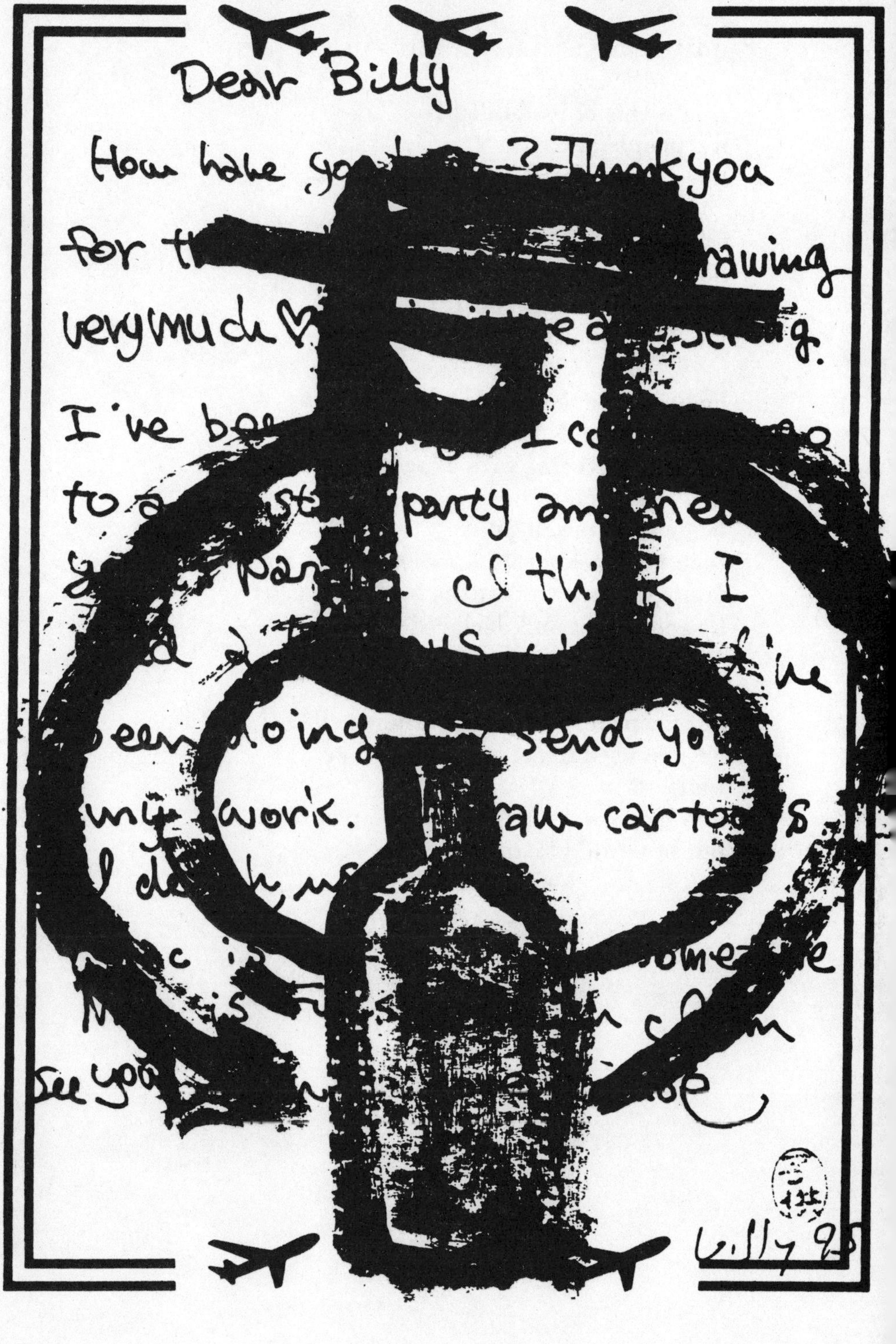
Dear Billy
How have yo
for th
rawing
verymuch
I've bee
party
send yo
work.
raw cartoo
see you
billy 95

names

one knows me as attacker
another a saint
one calls me generous
another denounces me as fake
one knows me as modest
another as king of braggers

one calls me brave
another coward

one sees me smilingly
another as melancholic
one calls me truth teller
another a lier
one knows me as quicksilver
another calls me idiot
one calls me lover
another names me whore

no matter how hard he tries
billy cannot be all things
to all people

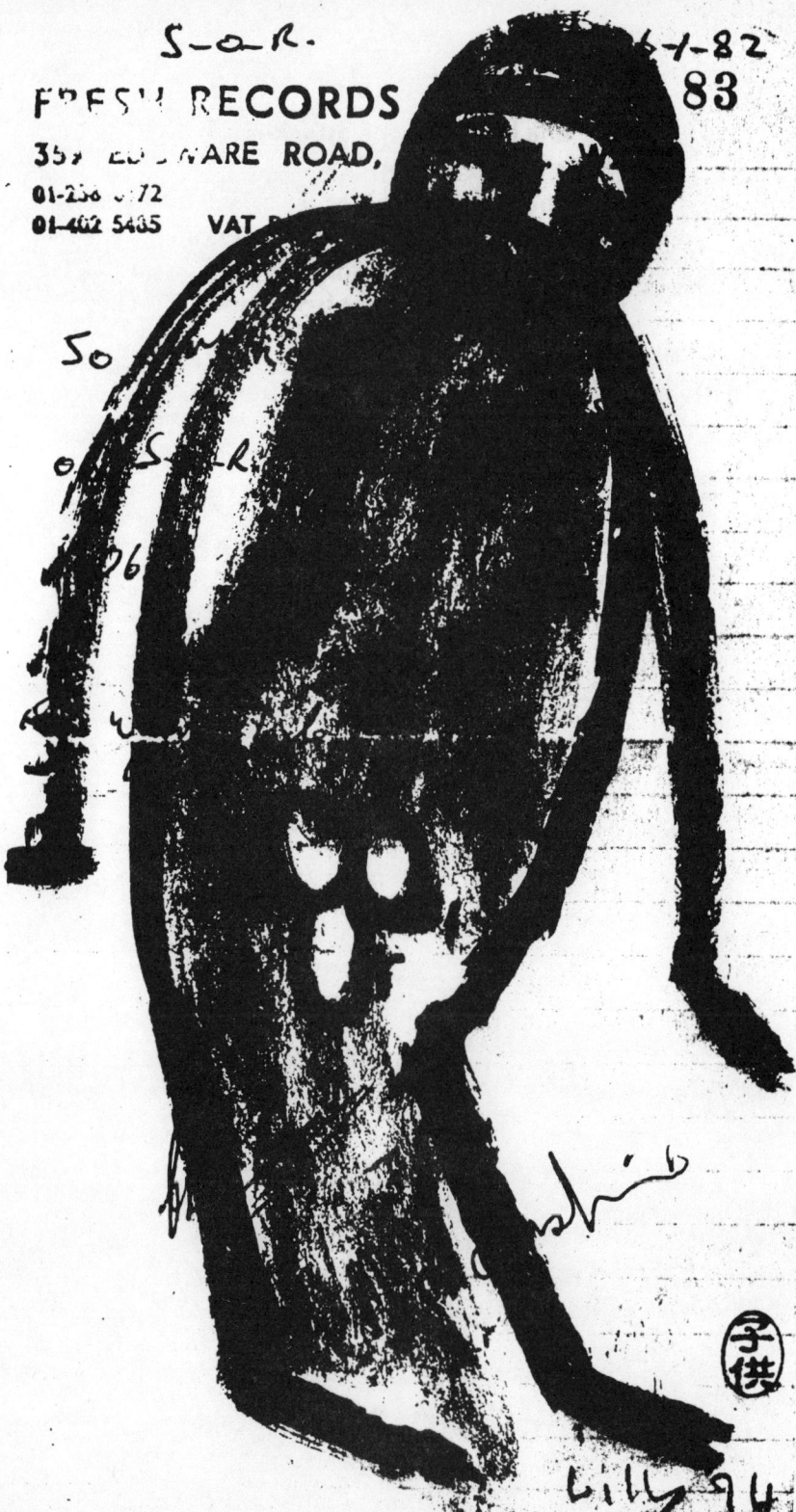

S-a-R.

FRESH RECORDS

35, EDGWARE ROAD,

01-258 072

01-402 5485   VAT

6-1-82
83

子供

Lilly 94

short changed

one even vowed to publish me
only to break his pledge
then stammering his excuses
moved on to publish another

it would seem that
ive been short changed
but in truth it is he
who has lost the chance
to serve me
to honour this man
this lonely werk

he has denied
none but himself

so whose loss is greater?
i am still here
grunting like a pig

HELLO! BILLY,

PURE FILTH WAS A L.A. BASED FANZINE
I HELPED OUT WITH, WE OR SHOULD I SAY
MY BEST FRIEND INTERVIEWED YOU. I
WANTED TO SEND YOU _____ BOOK SOONER
BUT AT ANY _____ HERE ____ ___ HOPE
YO_ __ ____ TAPE EVEN THOUGH I
THREW MY ____ICE OUT, AND I _OOK
ARTS·X. IT __S A BLAST BEING FEATURED
ON THE SAME _ SHOW 53 WITH PEOPLE
LIKE THE MU__IES, DAS KLOWN, RIP OFS,
FINGERS.

I WOULD ____VE KILLED __ WORK __TH YOU
ON THE ___ _ HA_US ____, HOWEVER
I WOULD ___ LIKE TO HEAR FROM YOU
IF YOU GET A CHANCE TO DROP
ME A LINE.

DIG IT TOUGH GUY

KERINE

(213) 257-552

P.O.B. 421064
YOUNG PERVERT
LA., CA 90042-1064

still bashing that banjo

im a living anachronism
i still rite poems
i still paint pictures
and im still bashing that banjo

im out of date
and out of touch
my contempories have all
past me by
whilst im still here experimenting
with coloured crayons theyve
all gone out and discovered
'modernism'

they walk around the playground
arms linked swearing like
six year olds whove just
discovered the word 'fuck!'
no wonder i feel left out

but even this little plot
of land they wont leave me
these purveyors of 'art-fashion'

says billy
i will stay here and
werk with my tools
and wait for this
merry-go-round to stop

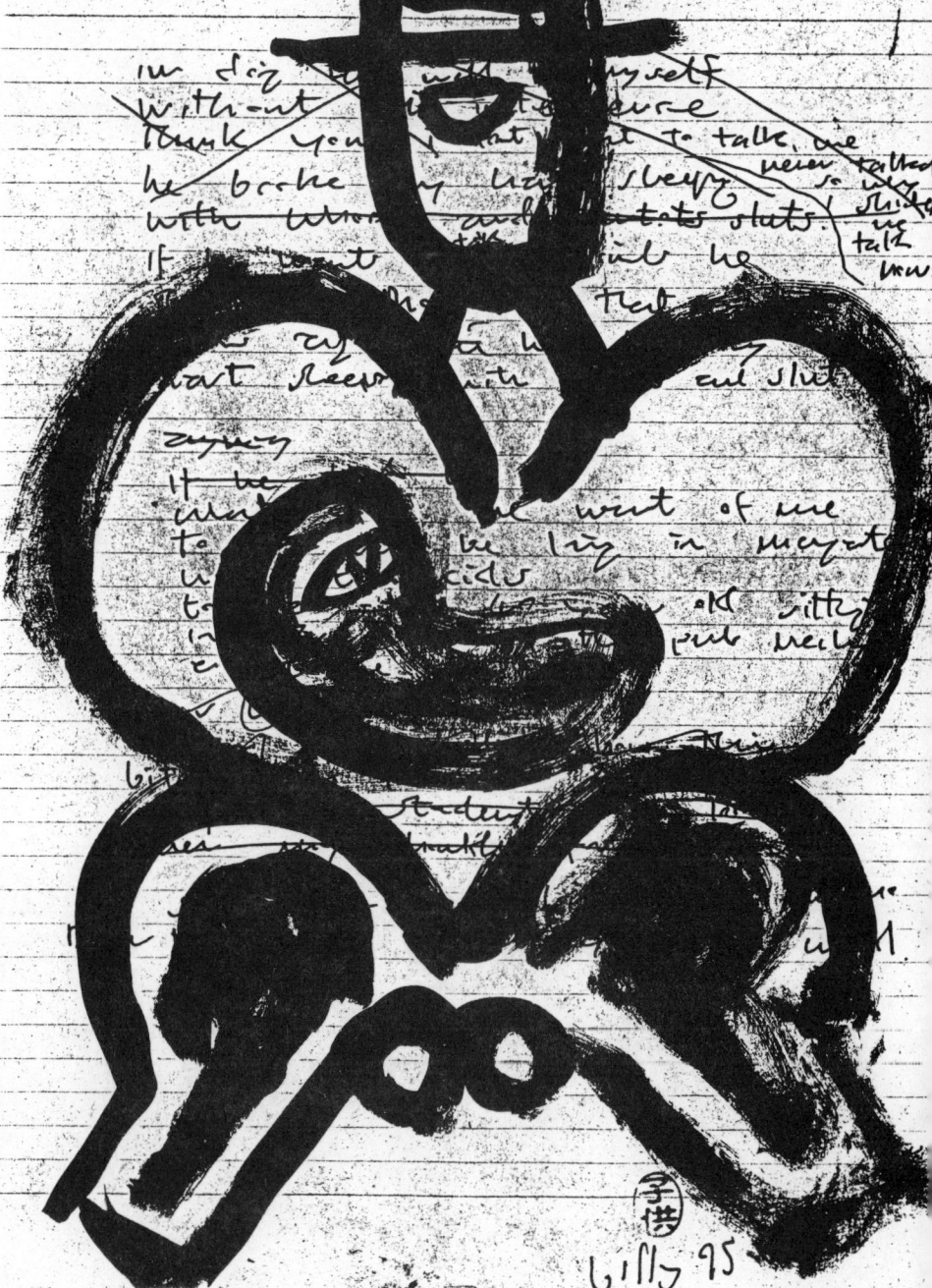

questions of originality

no matter how original
nothing can exist
that hasent breathed before

no matter how derivative
no idea can become
the model

therefor originality counts
for nill
all that we can do is swap
backgrounds
and startled the image is
seen afresh
and so the cliches fall

says billy
do not be intimidated by the junk
if it is brought into existance
then for what other purpose
than our use?

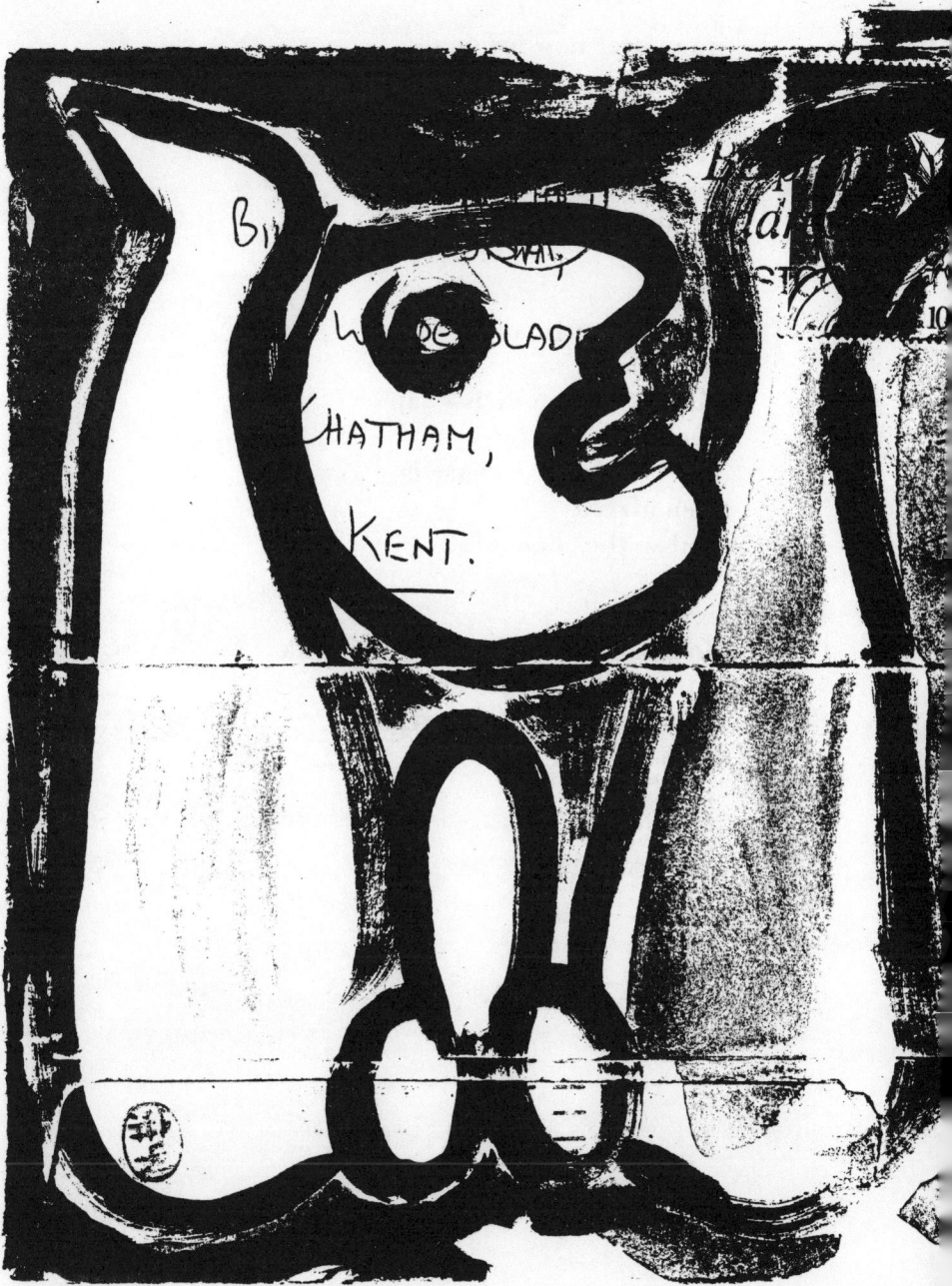

the class clown

i recognise this moment
as joyous
this constant turmoil of feeling
of bewilderment and unknowing

i stare at the buttocks of
strange girls
and in anger walk on
stumbling in wonder and
immaturity

so im not god yet
not jesus
not even a miserly saint

and i thought i was a
great artist!
a musician!
a poet!
but my reputation is
drawn in sand
a great philosopher fuck!
im nothing but a rookie
chewing gum in class
with everything to learn

says billy
its about time you quit
trying to be the class clown
and concentrated on your lessons

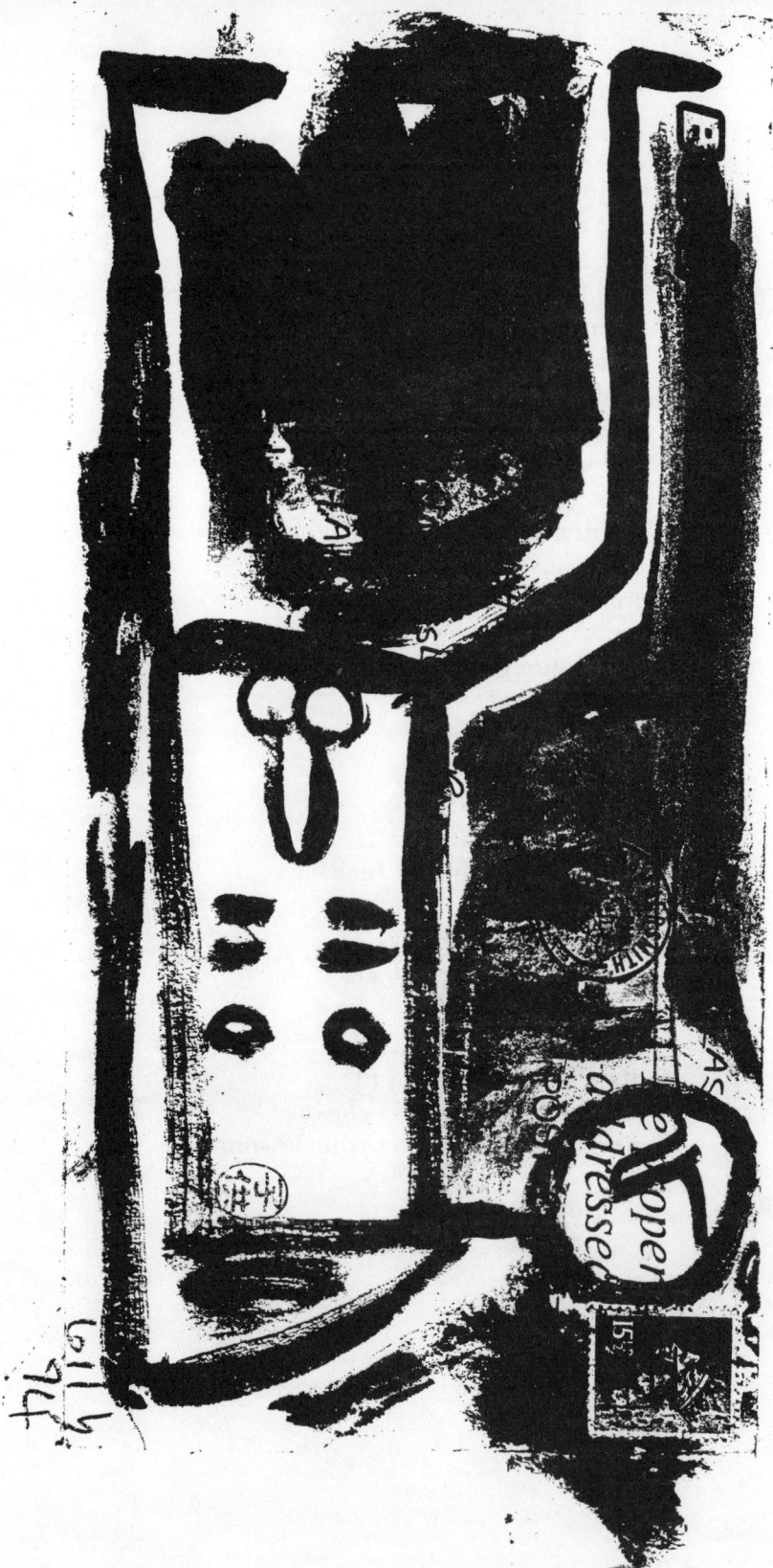

as wise as the
muscle of a dog

my great conceit
is to pretend that
ive always been
sitting here
that i am as wise
as the muscle of a dog

childrens hands wave
like flowers
and all other fellows
are second rate

ive drunk more than
any other
and pissed a reservoir
of love

ive ritten more
ive painted more
and fallen harder
than any other man

and ive always been
here
and ive always been
first
a tough nut
soft as shite

Principal Douglas May

Medway College of Design Fort Pitt

Our ref: RM/LB
6th December

Mr. S. Har___
181 Walde___ade Road,
Chatham,
Kent.

___ our last meeting on Thursday, 1st Dece___ with regard to
you___ttitude and progress throughout___ of the Foundation
Cou___. s it has ___ you during three previous
___ ___ ___ ember, October and November, and the advice
___ ___ members of staff during the term, we are unable to
support you___ ___tinued attendance after the Christmas vacation unless
there is a total ___ge in your attitude.

A Course t___at is structur___ ___o cope w__th 84 students must take into
consider___on the interest a___ ___jectives of the majority and it is
in protecting these interests ___ ___ ___ave found it necessary to call
into question your attitude of t___ ___ r___ection. In endeavouring to
come to terms with your particul___ ___ems we ha___ ___ffered you the
opportunity to replace the str___ ___ep programme with your own alter-
native but this has proved t___ ___ equally unproductive and ___ft you
free to continue disturb___ ___e other students on the C___ ___

Whilst I regret havi___ ___ take this action with any stu___ ___ I feel
it is now time for___ ___to make a decision either to wi___ ___ ___ ___ ___
Course or to ret___ ___ ___ accept fully the structure that ___ ___
through work r___cts for the remaining two terms. If yo___ dec___
to return u___ these conditions, I and the staff will re___ ___op
attitude ___ ___ ___ ___ evi___ce to support your cont___ ___ ___ have t___ ___ ___
our ___it___ ___ from the Course

You___

Reg M___le___
Head of ___ ___ ___mental Studies

someone else

someone else is holding this
someone else has ritten this
someone else has read this
someone else has thought this
someone else owns this
someone elses hands and eyes
someone elses breath
their fingernails trimmed
or broken

i can almost smell them
the taste in their mouth
someone else

on a single cheque but I haven't got many left.

I'm going to be in N.York for work from about Sept 22 - Oct 8 or so + I've thought it petty to show Jim Carroll + a few other (good) writers/poets here. In The meantime I HOPE the Makeshow article comes out + doesn't get botched up.

Again Thanks for your /Time/Patience/Interest/ Regards + best wishes + I'll talk to you on my return — Sorry This is hasty + written in The boat! (Hence grease spot!)

Cynthia Rose

brave little cinders

'you dwell on the past too much'
speaks my father in fear
'you dwell on the past too much'
agrees my brother
my mothers fingers flutter at her throat

above all my allegiance is to my family
and i serve them diligently
head bowed
never thanked
i serve them with love and respect

i am an old hag with one tooth in her jaw
i annoint my brow with ashes
no task is too wretched for me

through their denial i was forced to become
this chronicler
the harder the old man covers his tracks
the further my nose gets pushed into the grime
what they fear to utter
i will utter for them
what they cannot bear
i will bear in their place

my brother paints my pictures for me
for i have no choice but to paint what he omits
no matter how fast he runs
i call after him

ive been judged into non-existance
an untouchable
idiotised till im irrepressable
i am their holy fool
this smiling factotum

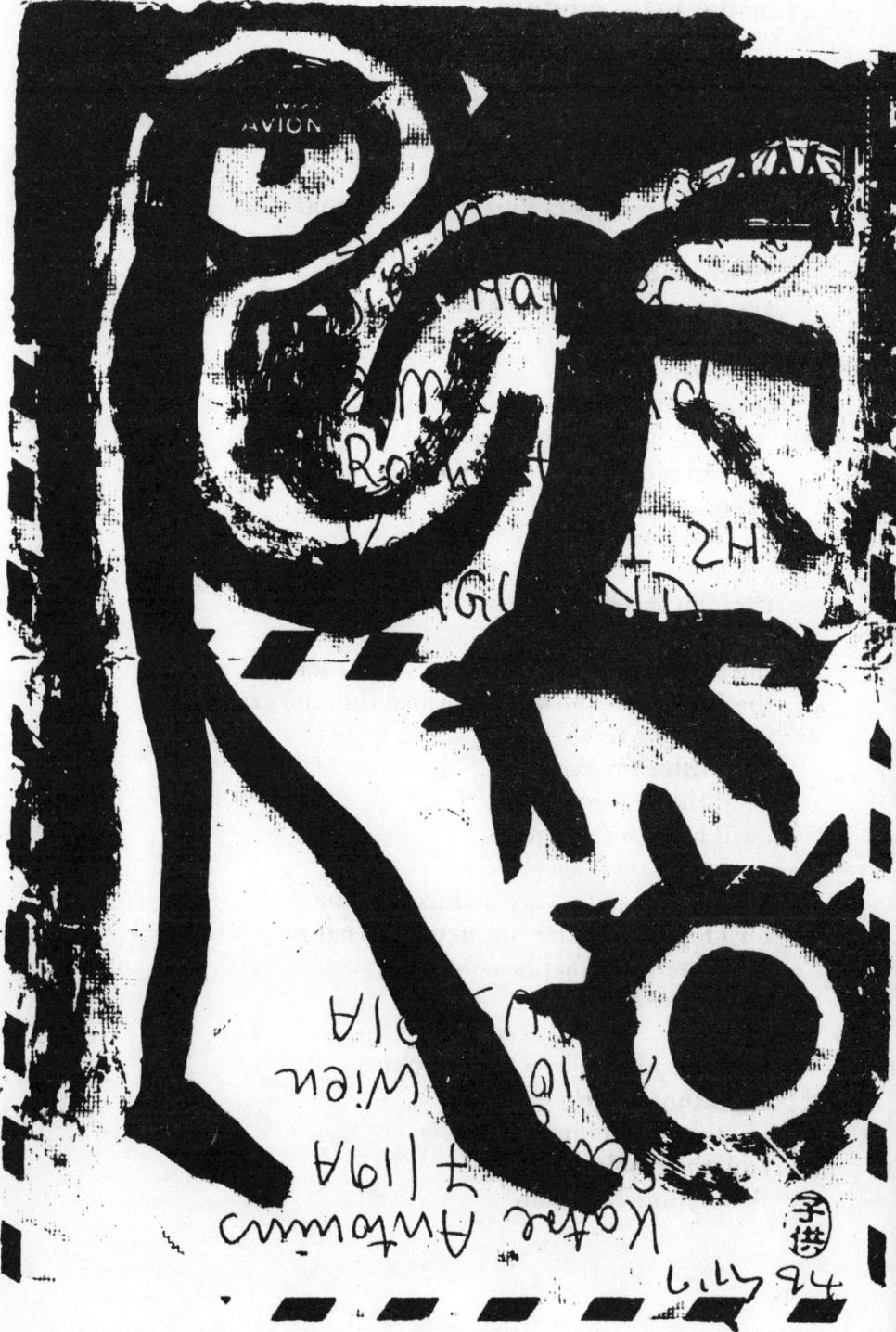

judging them all to hell

my friends arent good enough for me
my brother
my parents
my drawings
my paints
my house
this riting implement

no wonder the whole worlds up in arms
the poor bastards dont stand a chance
ive been judging them all to hell
they fail on every score
try as hard as they might
they can never come up to scratch

says billy
i will look instead to myself
and examine my own shortcomings
im strong enough for that too

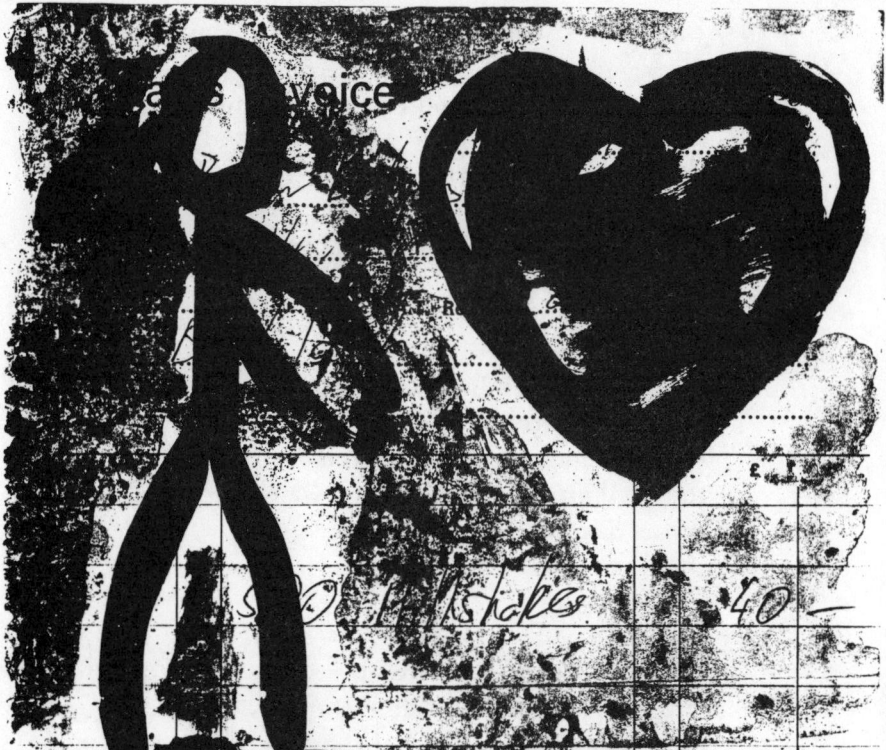

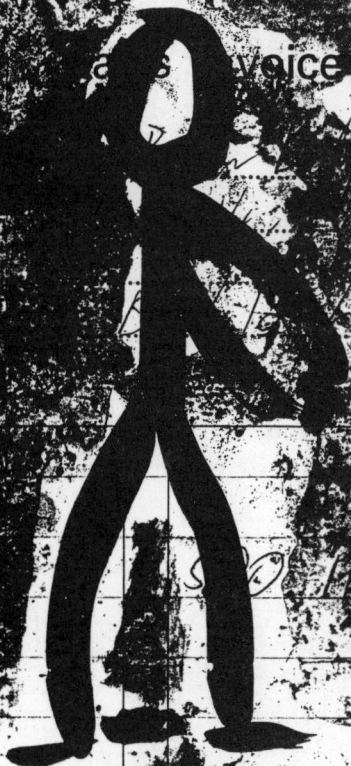

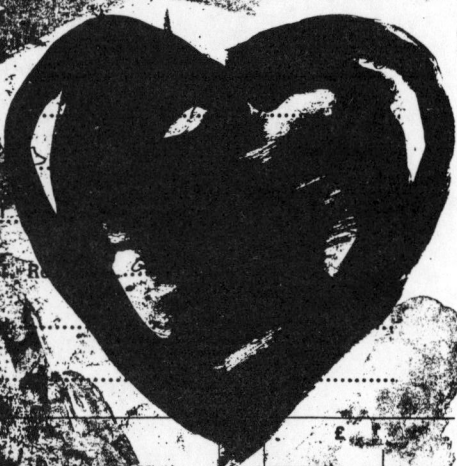

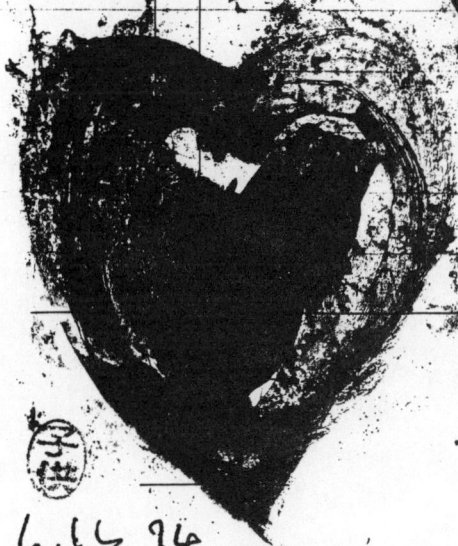

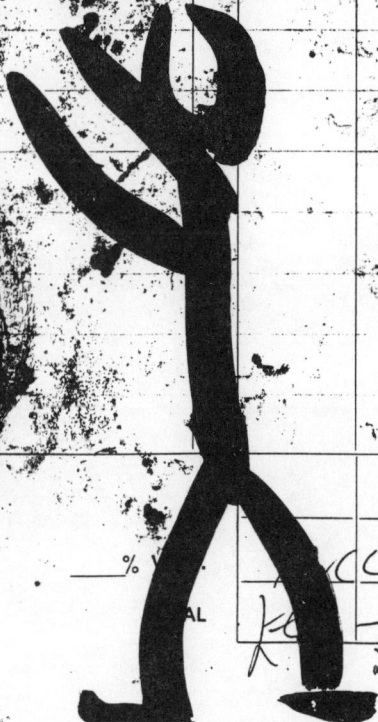

cease fire

brother
i call a cease fire
this province is
at peace

i will quit judging you
and learn only to love
that part of me
that you occupy

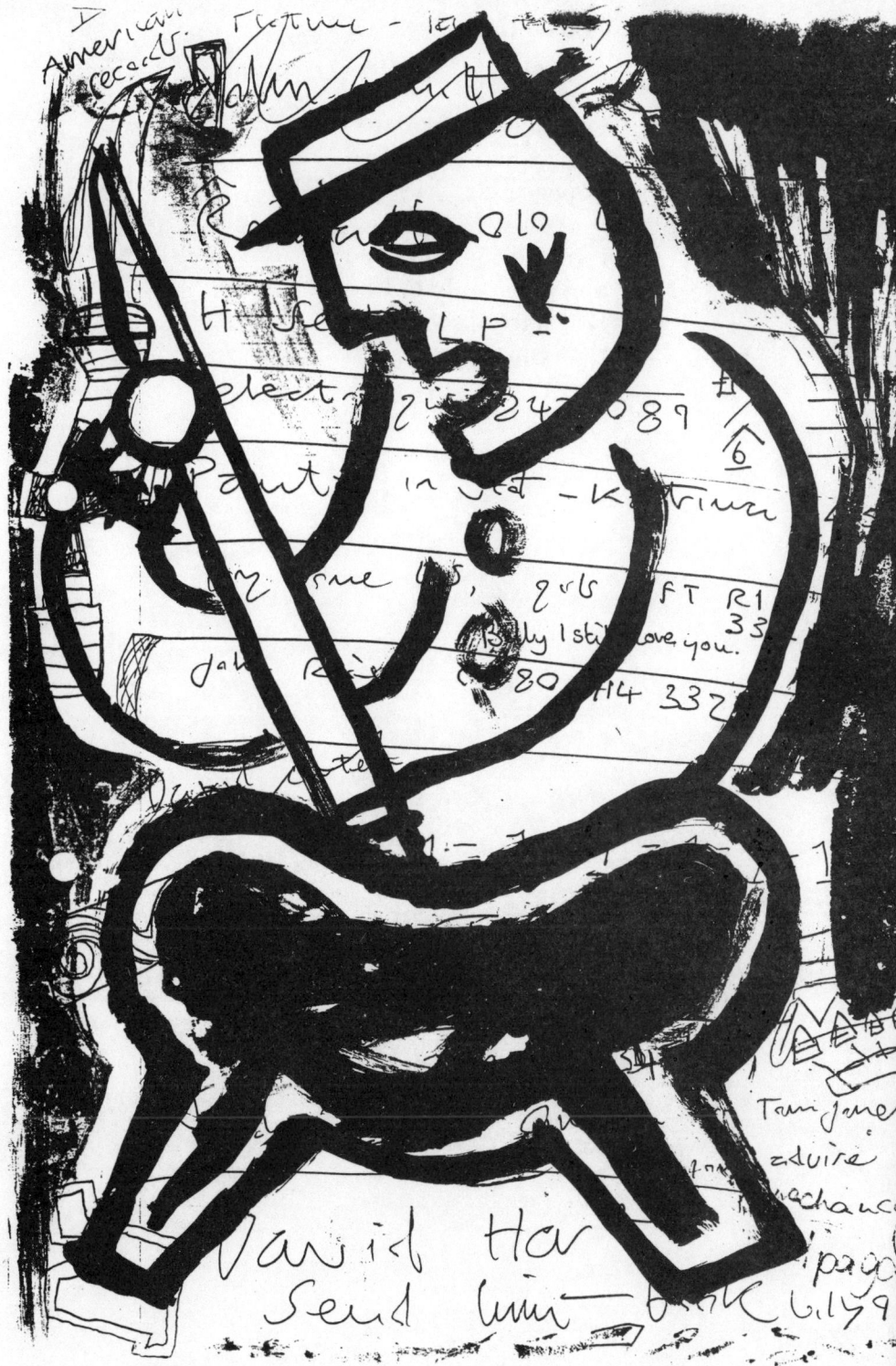

factotum

to tell the truth
this job is the pits
stigmatised for dirtying
my hands
on behalf of a society
of cowards

i should sweep roads
clean drains
and unblock sewers

i should hang a man
of their denial
before i rite this

pleased as punch

pleased as punch
i recount a childhood
of abuse and oppression

holding up my hart as
a rosy target
mocked and kicked all
the way
feared of hard werk
and a scrounger off
the state

its true
im as filthy as they come
ive conned the lot of you
but myself more than most
im a masturbator
my reputation is built on vanity and
falsehoods
my achievements blotted out
by my insatiable hunger
for praise

i cant imagine why you
love me

i dropped a tenner in
a beggars hat
hoping that god mite
bless me
but whose money is it anyway?
my fathers?
my countrys?

i make no sacrifices
i stuff my own face first
and put a little stash aside for later

i buy new clothes
and a dress for my wife
i get drunk and fall down
and punch a wall

listen
this is as it is
as i say it
my own broken truth

says billy
i cant undersand why
you even bother
to entertain me

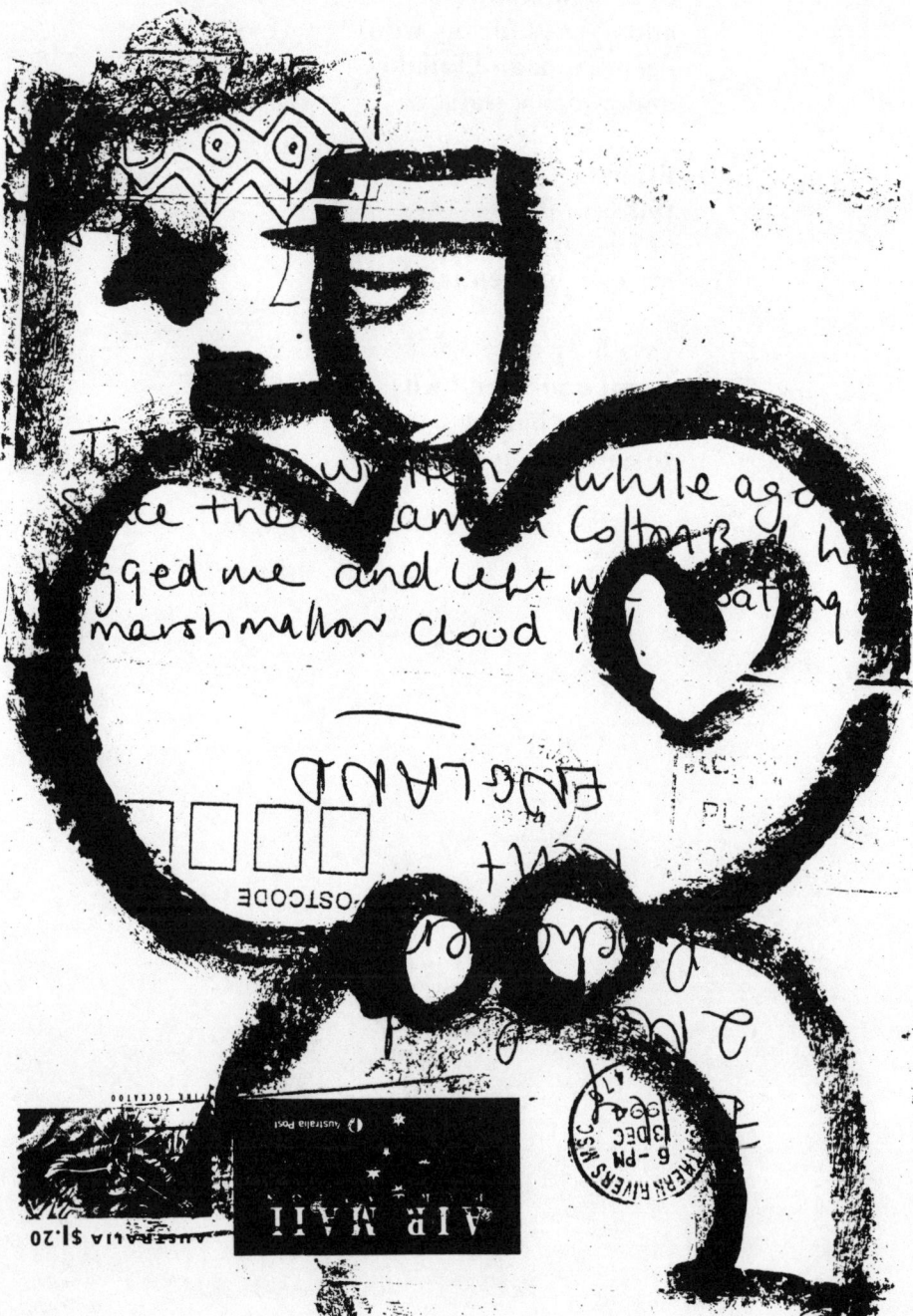

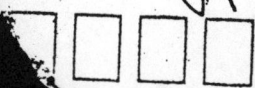

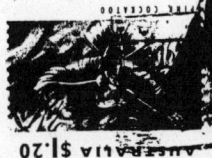

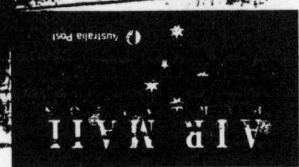

big balls and hart to match

i am a damaged man
ive been a damaged man
a damaged man dripping with
passion and guilt
damaged by my hunger for porn
and orgasm
with big balls and a hart to match

i call my deceipts unto me
come up from down below
and show your sun starved faces
for you are mine and you are dear to me
hand in hand shoulder to shoulder

come anger sit down by my side
and you greed i own you
quick come hither
and you my fear of god you are mine also
you fit me like flesh

i am a damaged man
ive been a damaged man
a damaged man dripping with
passion and guilt
and i dont know the meaning
of what i rite
but you will sucker me
for i am hungry for your truth

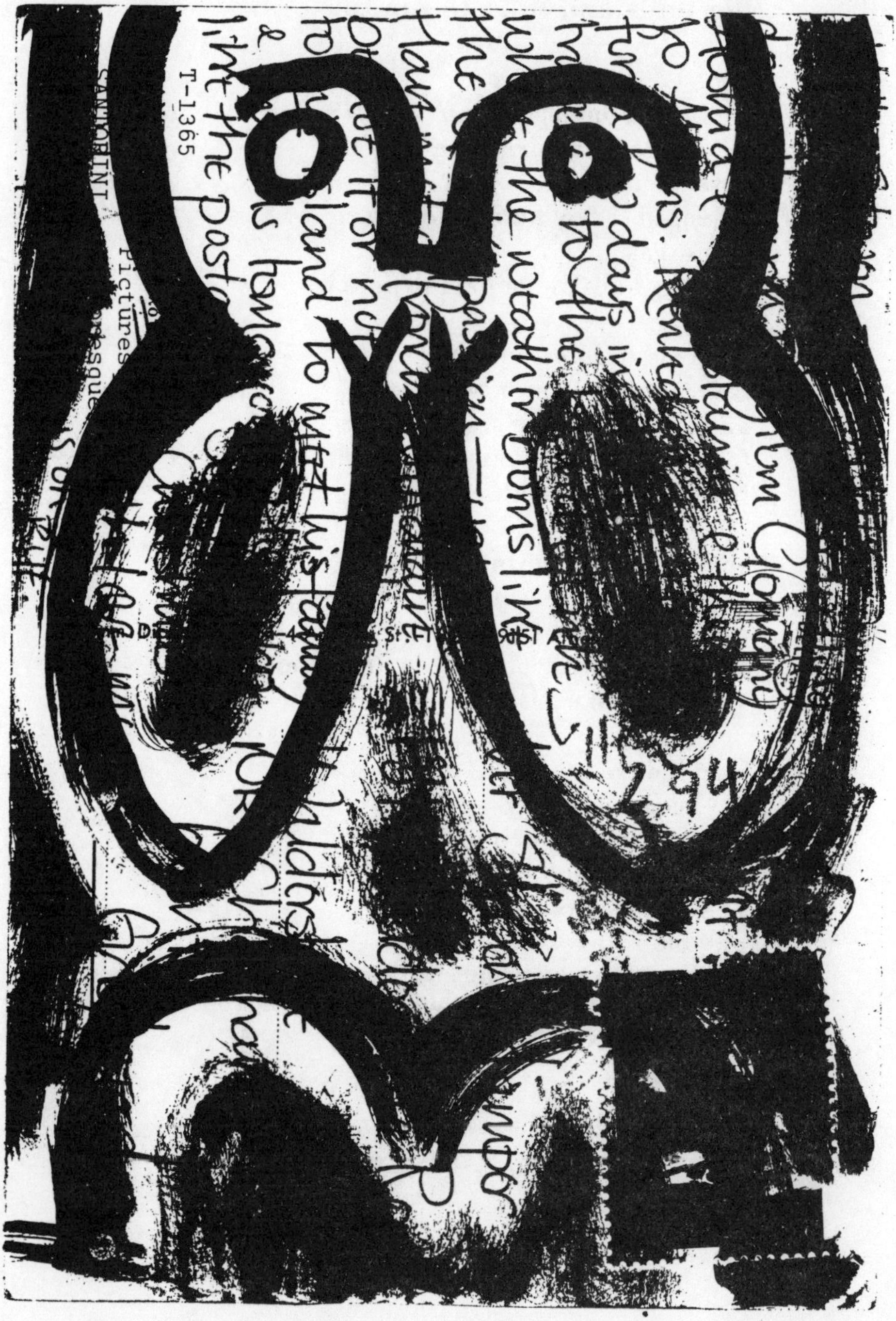

a dog dies

the tyer bursts
you receive a punch up the bracket
your house is broken into and
your possessions scattered
god is smiling on you

a whore robs your dole cheque
you receive a dose of the clap
a veil drops
god is smiling on you

your girlfriend quits you
your liver is shot
your tongue is cut
a reason is lost
god is smiling on you

your teeth are fucked
your ankle snaps
the phone is bust
a dog dies
god is smiling on you

a friend is lost
the day is bust
a fist closes
you are drunk of it
god is smiling on you

MR. & MRS.
& KYRA CHILNISH
HAY ROAD
ROCHESTER
BRITAIN

SEMRA KAYA

PTT Üst Sokağı No.3 AYDIN Tel: 0-256-225 61 43

MUHSIN ERTUĞ

TÜRKIYE CUMHURIYETI
10000 LIRA

the page of love

mend and sow
draw with these words
knit a unity

let the ink flow
the letters dance
and the s's smile

here is peace for
broken princesses
for the gun-wed
and de-harted

here is bandage
for bludded thoughts
and breast to calm
all maladie

where sister meets
brother
where brother holds
sister
and each knows
the rite to hold
themselves in love

Dear miss you

I L Y

I need you so much

Jeannine 11 years

2/17/94

the day knows itself

the day announces itself
with a fart
the day is barking
like a dog

knowing itself
it seeks itself
finding itself
it births itself

the nite announces itself
with a fart
the nite is barking
like a dog

WALL TO WALL
T·E·L·E·V·I·S·I·O·N LTD

Blackhand Distribution
Rd.
Roch
Ken
ME 1 2HY

GREAT BRITAIN
≈ 19 ≈
HB 48133 C
POSTAGE PAID

LONDON
20.IX.94

2 may rd

a windswept terrace
atop a hill
owned by a never seen
polak in southend

no heating
four sticks of furniture
the front door buckled off
its hinges
and a cellar full of noise

then the lady from the agency
saw me grinning on tv
that impressed her
'cut your hedge!'
she ordered
'and tidy up that back yard!'

but this house is
stashed with paintings and guilt
poetry upon poetry
and ive been happy here
these past eleven years

some terrible lies
have been lived here
and a smattering of love

says billy
i must leave to find out
if i exist beyond my werk

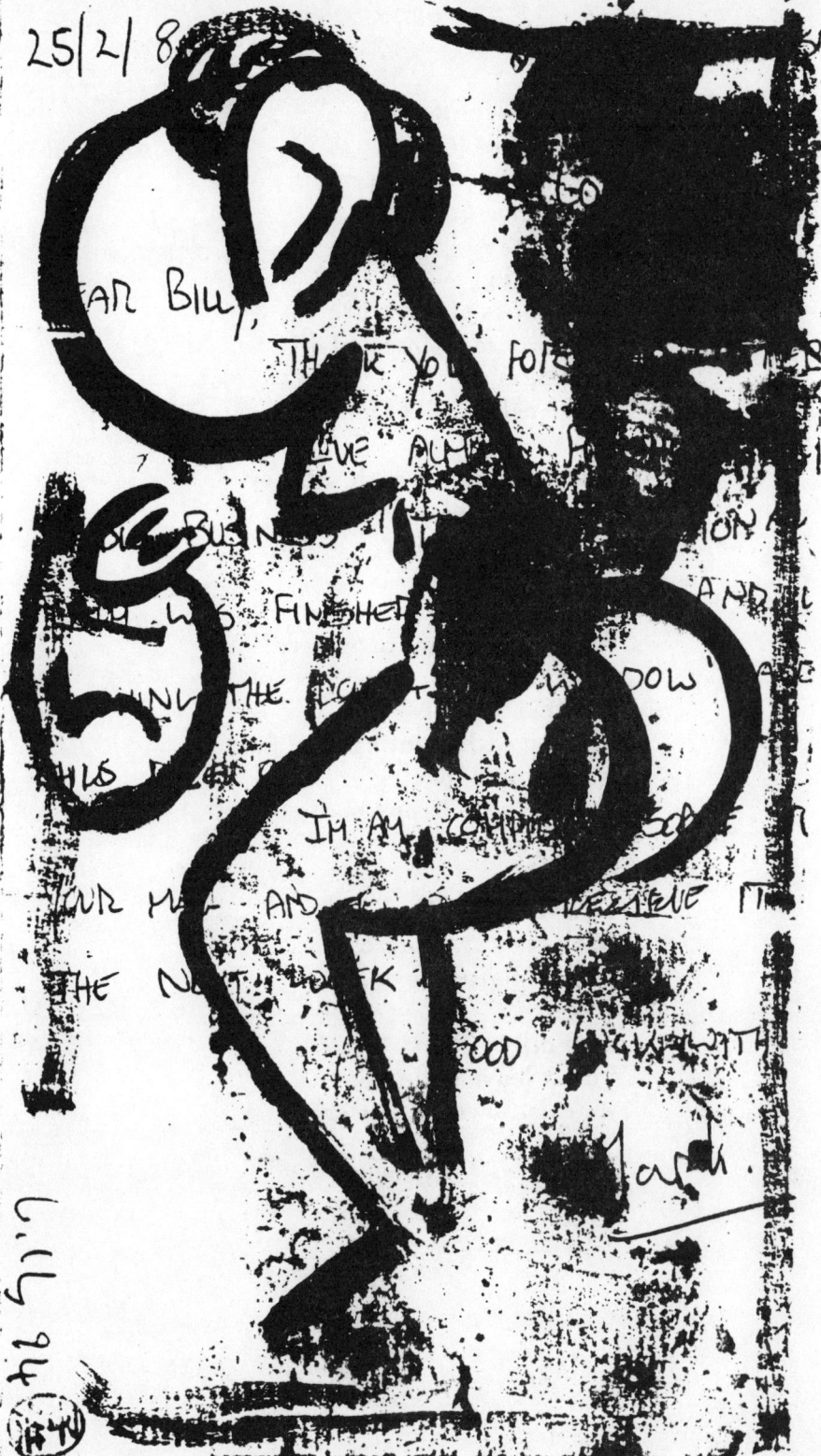

paper whores

dreams are for sale
butiful dreams
desperate dreams
and every lost little hart
is eager to be hooked
into them

i too could be this butiful
to own this car
this woman
this dream will sustain me
at least for the magical
moment when hot coin
passes from palm to palm

i will be forfilled
i plead to the paper whores
i will be forfilled
i cry to the till girls
i will be forfilled
i scream at the galleries
at the artists down the ages

i will be forfilled
i mouth silently
at these advertising hoardings

yes
this will be me
i will be caught in time
just like these heroes
and be honoured held and
loved

says billy
quit this obsession you
mad person
the illusion of time has hold
of you

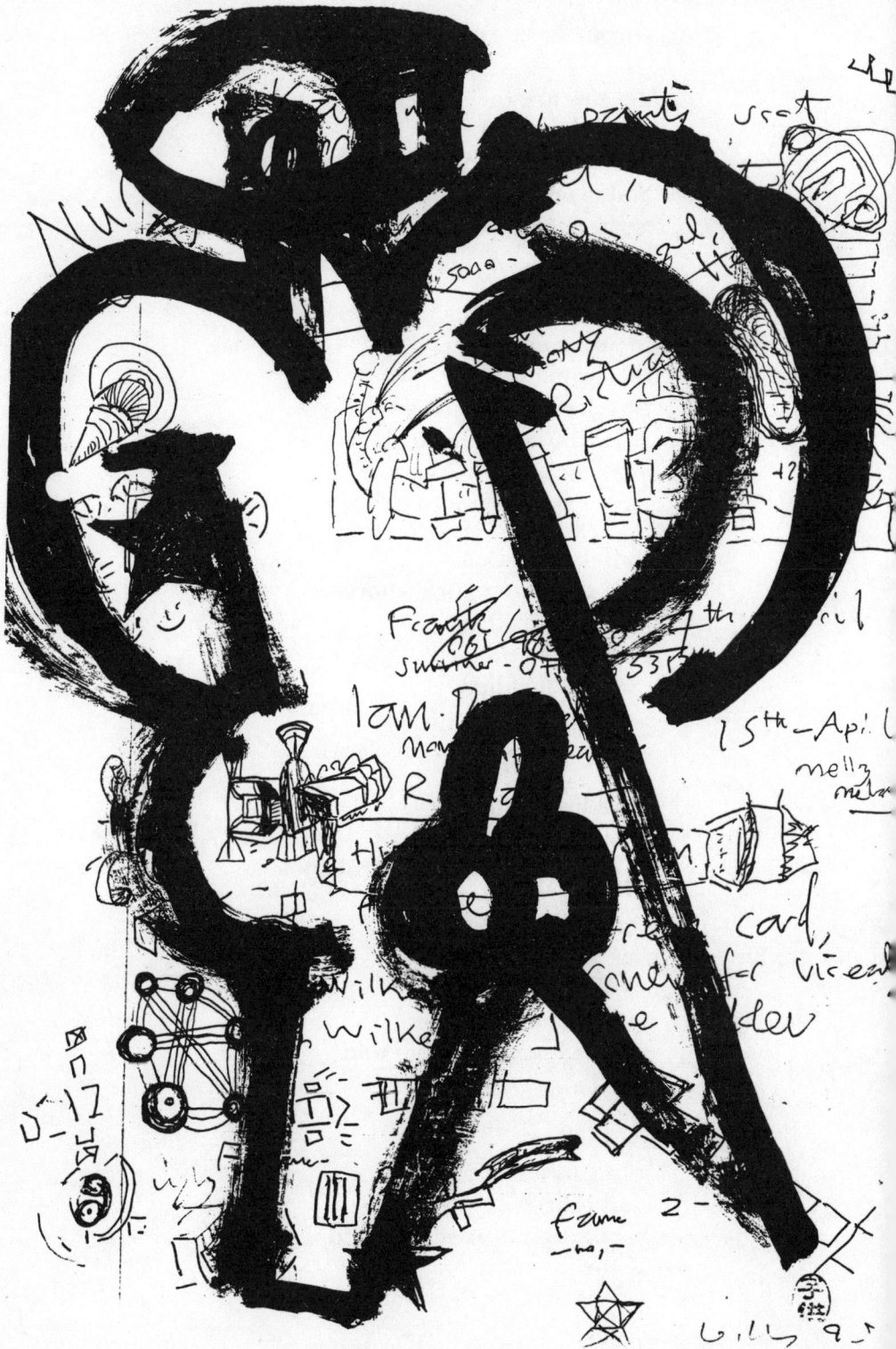

the naked poet

i am the naked poet
with blud in my cock
impudent as hell
emabarassing my poor peers

lately my style is all shot
to bits
my delivery stammering
but i hide behind no one

i rite verses for kings
for whores and thieves
everywhere
for my father and mother
with respect
for my brother with love
for brothers and sisters
unknown

asks billy
when oh when will i be accepted
or do i first have to
swallow myself whole?

From Traci 3d Castle Hill
Rochester.

S.W.A.L.K.

Mr B Chadwick
2 Lay Bye
Rochester
Kent

Gillo 94

poems for a pissed off wife I
(with thanks to tuka)

he thinks hes got it sussed
that hes worldly wise
that hes been out there
and experienced life
but in truth he knows fuck all!

i have to treat him with
kid gloves
he isnt big enough to take
the message

his paintings are stuck stuck stuck!
he is stuck!
still playing that stupid music
and riting those idiotic poems

says billy
dont you know that ive travelled
to the four corners
that ive conquered self-loathing
hatred of the world
and king alcohol
and not by denial you bitch
but walking clear through
to the other side

Sunday night,

... childish,

... a ... y ... letter of
sorts ... cause I ... Nicko talk...
to you ... I ... I want to
say ... I ... as ...

It's ... uckin time ... ha...
mum ... come ... ...
special ... ... they
Sunday ... 81 ... was roast
chicken ... blackberry &
apple p... ... s... vice, but
old,

... I feel ra... ... moment,
... I feel most... ... ... ,
nowadays ... ... that
... ... then
mats ... ...
the fear of ... no ... too-
cautious,

=I did same drawing this
f s (⊙)

poems for a pissed off wife II

if he wants to talk and
be friends
he should have thought of that
eight years ago
before he broke my heart
sleeping with whores and sluts

what does he want from me?
to still be living in margate
with two kids?
to be fourty years old sitting
in the corner of the pub
necking a bottle of cider?

says billy
stupid bitch
do you still not know
that you paint your own world

As pooring with rain now, really
miserable ... night ...
tow ... for a walk
... ther
... And ... er so tired
so ... ake a cup
... tea ... to bed, I hope
I go ... perly, I was
a bit ... last night, sorry
scr,
... I say nonight,
I ...

P.c. look ...
terrible ...
cal did find it,

poems for a pissed off wife III

ive grown ive changed
im not the same as i was back then
he cant talk to me like im a stupid
eighteen year old school girl anymore

but still he keeps on trying to bully me
he wants to talk but i dont want to talk
i dont want him any closer
whats wrong with arguing?
weve always argued
im happy with it like it is
i dont want a closer relationship

says billy
you claim to be different
and that you have changed
but you dont want anything to change

muddled woman
please shoulder your responsibilities
or again youll leave it all to me

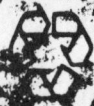

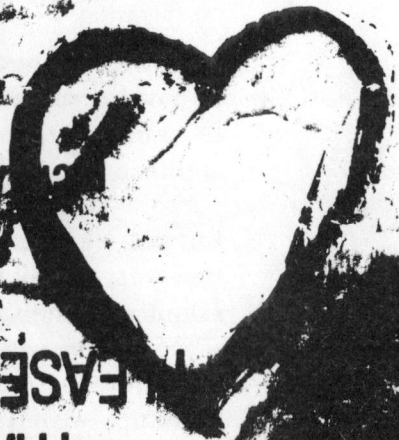

she looks down

she moves in the circle of art stars
and looks down on people who
'do not forfill their potential'

'my books sell for a hunderd and fifty pounds each
and ive sold a hunderd and twenty of them'
she simpers
'my friend is giving a talk at goldsmiths college
about her werk tonite her nose stuffed full of coke'

'how many does she have to convince of her greatness
before she is satisfied?'
asks billy
'only one'
he answers himself

Bill Harper
2 May Road
Rochester
Kent

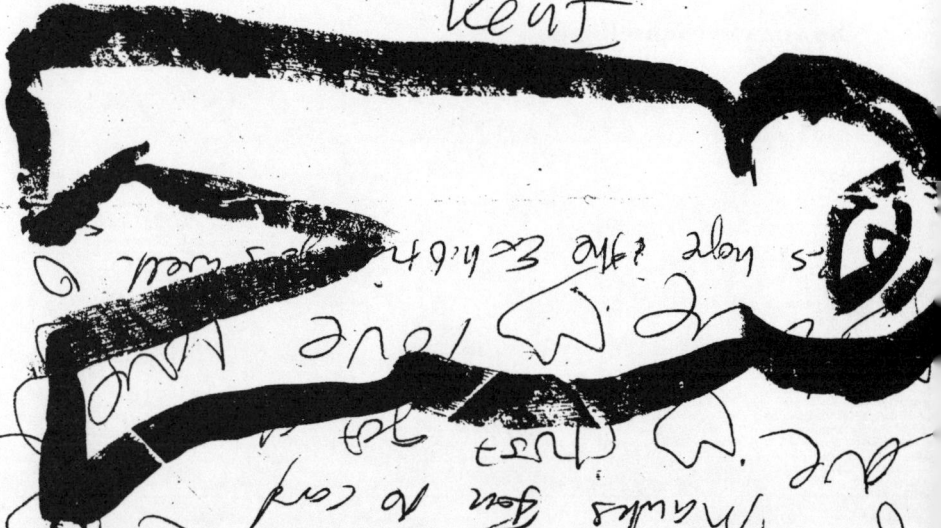

Thanks for 10 card
Sweet pea
world hates
yes to whole bloody
love
love
love
Lilya

waterloo station

ive been ill
i was ill all last year
i split up with chris
i had an abortion
it was twins and
they cut them up inside
of me
and two days later
a little arm came out
whilst i was sitting
in the taxi
but i wont tell you
about it cos youll
only go and blab about it
in one of your stupid poems

she glared at me
hungry and broke
and i understood
that what i loved about
this woman
was the depth of her spite
and anger
she hated the world
she hated men
and she hated me

i handed her a twenty
and watched her stupid
face light up

shell remember all of my
indiscreditions
but never the gift
of this poem

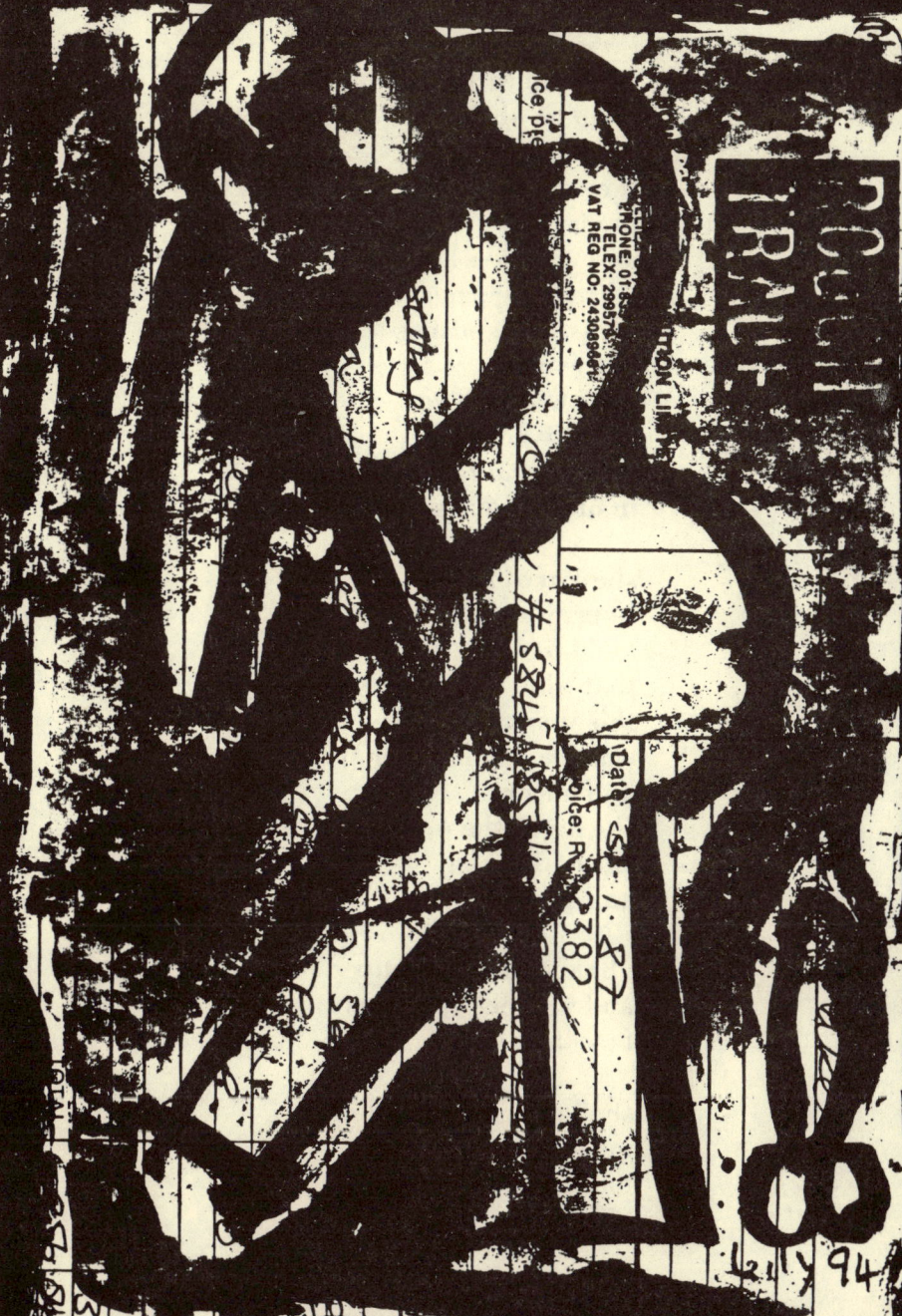

the poem as revenge

no secret is safe with me
do not trust my smiling eyes
i am the king of indiscretions

how often ive used the poem
in revenge
hunting down my opposition
using my humour as bludgeon

and why must i always be in revenge?
to lower her
to break her tilted jaw
so grand she has grown
she papers her shit house
with her degrees

once i controlled her
it took all of my efforts
for two solid years
but no more
now i let go...

this poem is nothing but
my bitterness at not
being able to stop the world

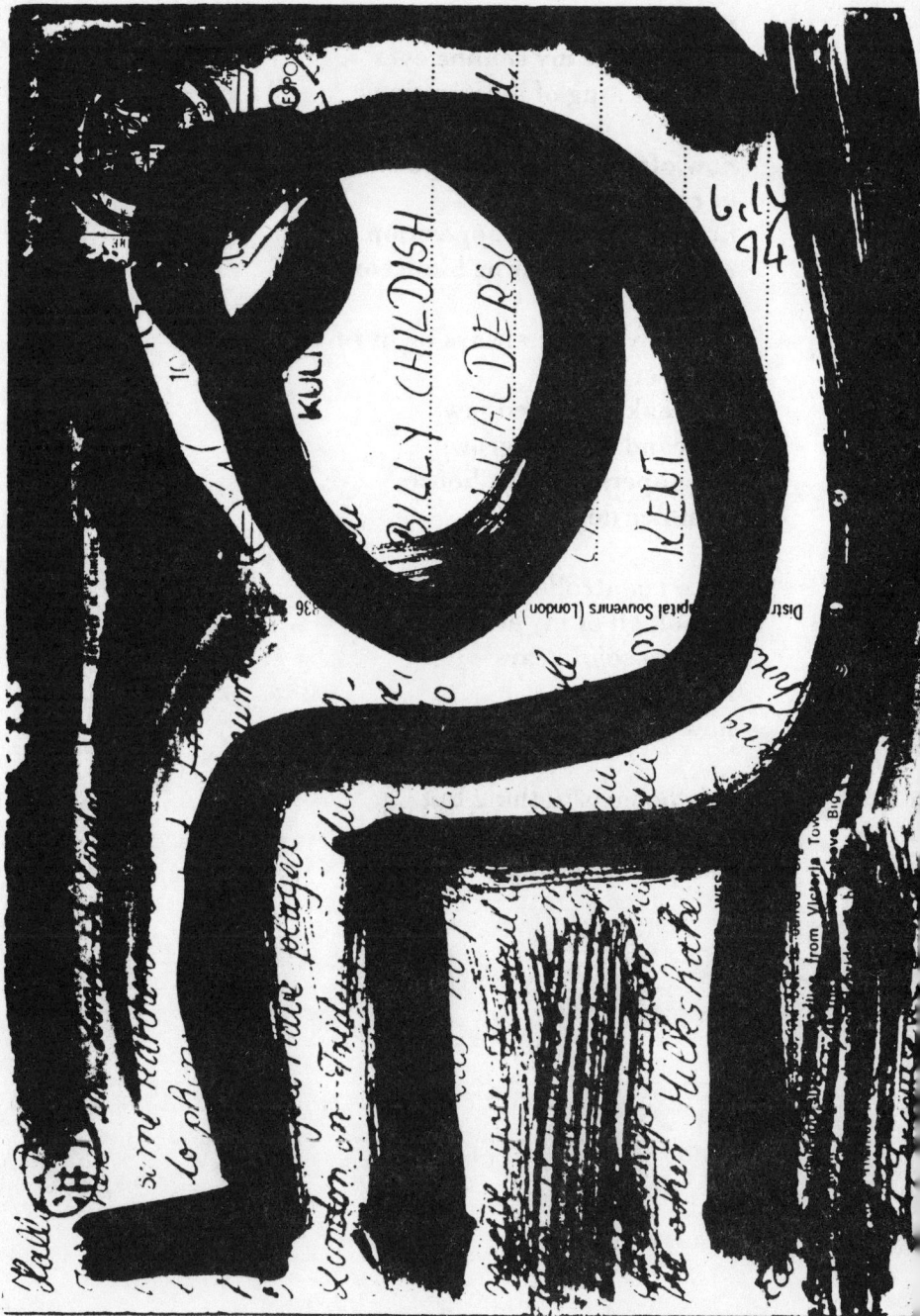

BILLY CHILDISH

WALDERSL

KULI

KENT

billy
94

all my friends ive hurt

ive been labeled
and labeled myself to hell
heavy with obsessions
pummeling my poor hart
out of existance

and all my friends ive hurt
my mother
my father
my poor family
ive labeled them all
as arseholes

it seems that ive been
indiscreet
babbling our misfortunes
on the streets
battering my lovers
into silence
till even god goes
schtum on me

and now i reap the pain
gauging to the very quick

asks billy
is there no depths
i wont sink to
to know myself?

SIGN ON MONDAY
Pick up RA.
letter to
Tiger in your tank.
Full blown ja! Hunger-
T + Barge.
Publish
3rd sept,
one were.

completely brave

the judgments of others
find vicious echoes
in my own uncertainty

says billy
one must indeed be brave
to let go ones position
completely

Dear ...

I think that ... ... her ... and.
I think that ... ... your ...
are wrong — I ... ... wish that you
just believe me — I hate to ... ... happy —
there is no reason for you to be
... I'm not with you ... about you
really mean it.

I know you think that I don't really care
... you - but I do. I think youre so nice, I
really want you to like me too.

I don't know how I can show you that what
I say is true and that I really like you a lot

Anyway - I'll be seeing ... minutes and
I hope ...
that ...
feel ...
... that I
... real
...
at - ... ... Billy-
just ... ... feeling
unhappy.

Please don't ever think that I'll try to turn you
away - I never will, whatever happens I'll

an offering or a bonfire

how shall i ever repent
for the evil i continually rite
for the anger and the passions
that i eagerly arouse

who is there to punish me?
should i go down upon my knees
and make an offering
or a bonfire?

asks billy
will i ever manage
to forgive myself?

Dear William,

Thank you for your completed application form for the Vipassana Meditation Course to be conducted by ... assistant teacher(s) to S.N.Goenka, at Dhamma ... wood End, Hereford. A place has been reserved for you on the course. ... for ... you ... able to attend please let us know as soon as possible, so that your place may be given to someone else. The course will start on the ... 23rd Dec ... and finish on the morning ... (9 ...) Please arrange to arrive between 1 ... and ... pm on 27 ... (please note: It is not possible for New students to stay overnight at the ... course begins.) Registration will take place during the afternoon ... meal will be served in the evening ...

HOW ...

Dhamma ... ted 2 miles from the village of Harewood End between Ross-on-... and Hereford (6 miles). From Harewood End take the second ... the bottom of a hill just before the ... sign for Hay-on-Wye (B43 ...) at the second crossroads turn right, signposted 'Dhamma D... ... area ... on the back of this sheet. ... er travel details including ... train times are included ... separate sheet.

WHAT TO BRING

Bring all your own warm bedding requirements i.e. sleeping bag, sheets and a pillowcase. Pillows will be provided. ... cushion ... dining ... and a shawl. Bring warm and comfortable clothing, paying ... to the section headed 'Clothing' in the Code of Discipline ... Note that leggings are not suitable worn ... own. The ... with skirts or knee length tops. Also bring slippers ... are limited. Bring a towel and your own ... Please note that Dhamma Dipa is a rural property. You are ... bring warm and waterproof clothing and ... boots.

PLEASE DO NOT BRING ...

... uables, books, religious ... musical instruments, tape recorders and ... ting materials.

... th kind regards,

advice from god

my meditations
are crap
i fart rite the
way thru
from begining to end
and
think of nothing
but pornography
and sex

my little god
hardly gets to say hello
he carnt hear himself think
above the roar

he holds his nose
and shouts
'please
think of your soul
of your enlitenment
and
for pittys sake
quit scribbling that
junk all the time'

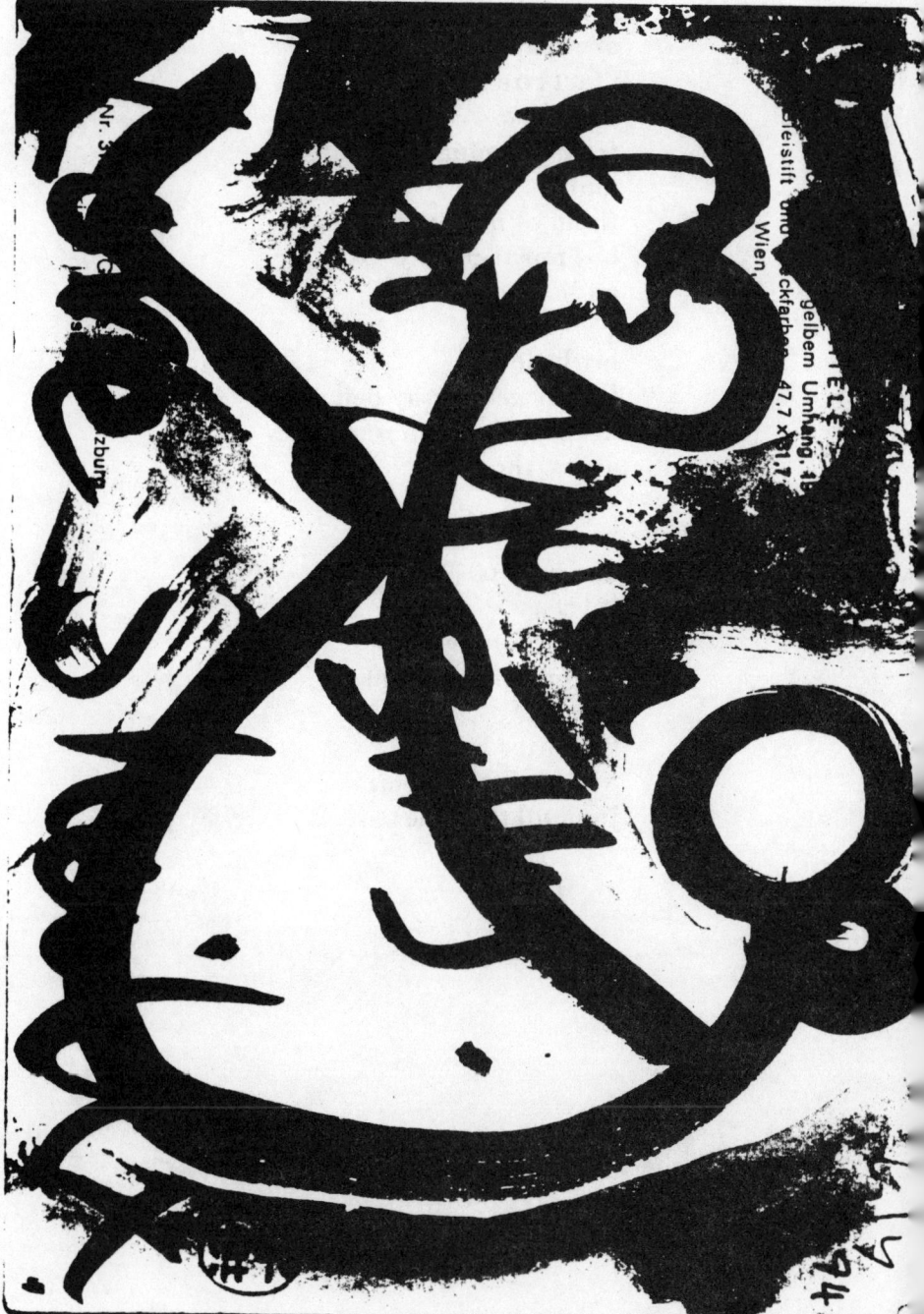

acid based flux
bakers fluid

this is the path
everything is the path
and all walk upon it
knowingly or unknowingly

there is no loss here
only opportunity
nothing is of value
and even the fear and lies
build truth

each moment is
deadly with sorrow
and seriousness
to be laughted at
and dropped

for nothing can be
held in this flux
this moment naked
again and again
and everything is the path

DN. 1998

Pablo PICASSO (1881-1973)
Le chap... feuillage bleu
Juan-...
huile...

15½ P

c. barain

fresh and wise

always it seems
that i am back at square one

was a time i did nothing
but sex and drink
i was renowned for it
honoured in my stupor

'he will curse and fall down
in a minit
all you have to do is
sit and watch'

and now ive dropped
the bottle
but still i stagger
drunk on self
i turn into a gourmet

i must eat i shout
pushing my way to the trough
im seeking god says billy
wishing to be known
as fresh and wise

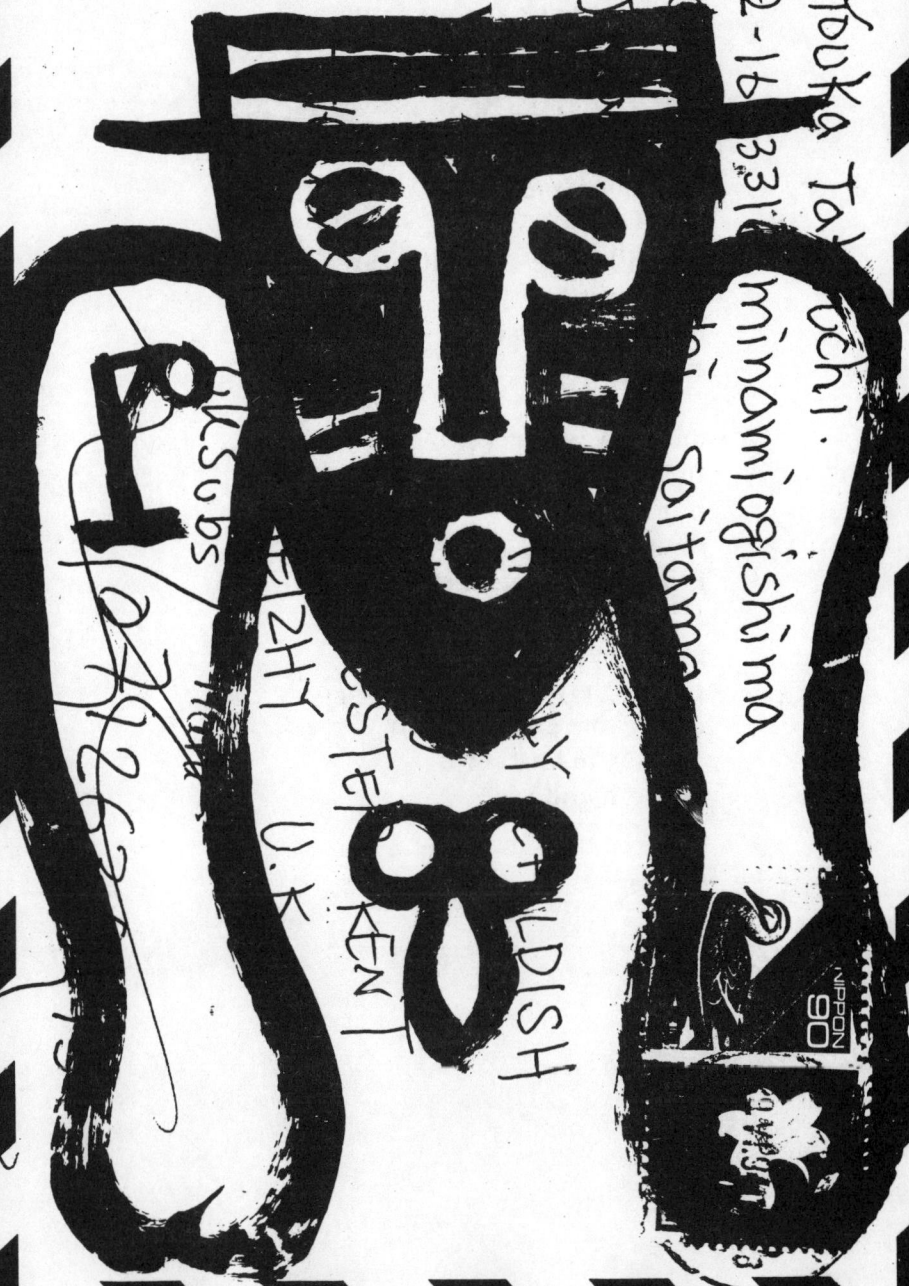

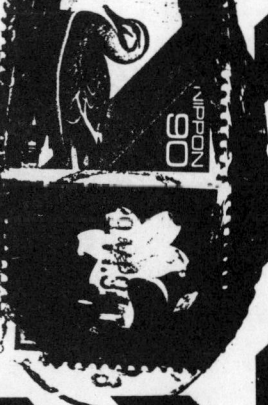

badges of hell

i etched this flesh
with stubborn badges
drawings of the damned
and cigarettes stubbed
to the quick

to be loved
and honoured is what i needed
to be aknowledged as god
to be breathed over
and held

but only fear held me
and the hands of lovers
that i could not believe

so i branded these pallid limbs
least others would brand me
and i hated myself
before any other could hate me

so when loathed i smile
for none can despise me
as sweetly as i despised myself

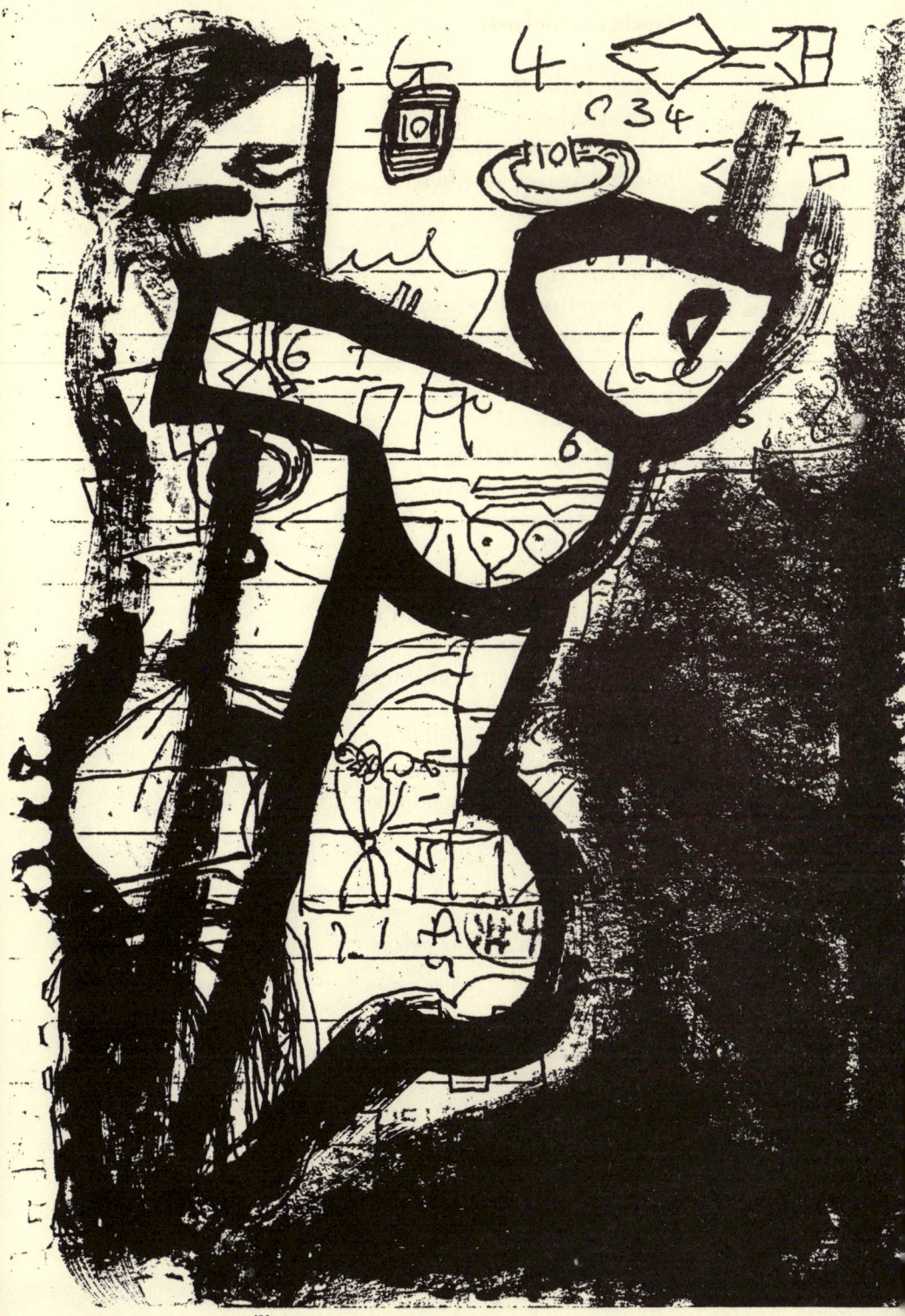

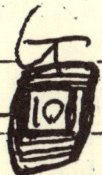

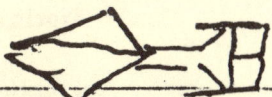

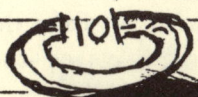

dreams of heaven from hell

forgive me if i appear
a little lost
but im riting myself
into existence

i cant let go the pen
or quit this babbling mouth
my eyes are everywhere
theyre as indecent as hell

damn them
ile pluck them out
and throw them
on the street
like oysters

actually i walk like a
teenager with a stiff dick
but afraid of every minge
i meet

says billy
dear god
i dont know what i deserve

INVOICE

HOME & GARDEN

BUILDERS and D.I.Y. SUPPLIES
GLASS - TIMBER - PLUMBING

122 DELCE ROAD
ROCHESTER, KENT

Tel.: MEDWAY 45740
VAT Reg. No. 373 6631 38

186

	2	70
	1	55
	6	32
		50

03886

another me

i dont drink
i dont smoke
i practice meditation
i go to bed early
i honour both my father
and my mother
i am vegetarian
and smile politely

my friends come round
the house
to laugh at me
they cover their mouths
or at least they ask
'what happened?
is there no hope?
no cure?'

and i smile
yet i am still me
this unknown man

says billy
it seems that there is
another me who calls
himself nothing

14700 Hollow Tree Rd
Orland Pk, IL 60462
USA

C/ ...gman Records
2 May R...
Rochest...
Kent
...England!

...y Childish

AIR MA...
AR AV...

29 JL
1994

USAirmail
50
...Quimby
Pioneer
Pilot

beneath the shit

so often i am overwhelmed
by this physical world
by its broken sights
and deafening sounds

how to admit to it all?
what truth is required?
and how to know that it is indeed
the truth?

knowledge can go take a walk
to hell with reputations
i have no decorum
god is not in heaven
heaven is in god
and god is within
smirking beneath the shit

TWO

I am trying to organise the publicity through the local press and,
once we know the venue I hope TVS can advertise the event.

I hope all this is OK. Please contact me if there are any
problems.

With good wishes

Gerry Harrison
Producer
GETTING IN

P... I hope the date — 25 March —
fits in OK before your Germany
schedule.

PPS. I'm going to check out the
YORK on Friday evening. Let
me know if you can come
down there.

PS. Liked the LP!

billy 94

half-wit

full of shame i share with no one
but shamed of nothing
i share this nonense with all

speaking the rong words
the rong sentiments
in the rong bars
in the rong pubs
to the rong faces

so i stand jaw clenched
i serve myself and swallow without chewing
then que-up for seconds

then sensing that im a half-wit
and suddenly knackered
i sit and meditate in agony
my back roped with knots

and so i call myself god
and i look to my hands with disbelief
it seems that ive judged all other down
and stepped on my own face

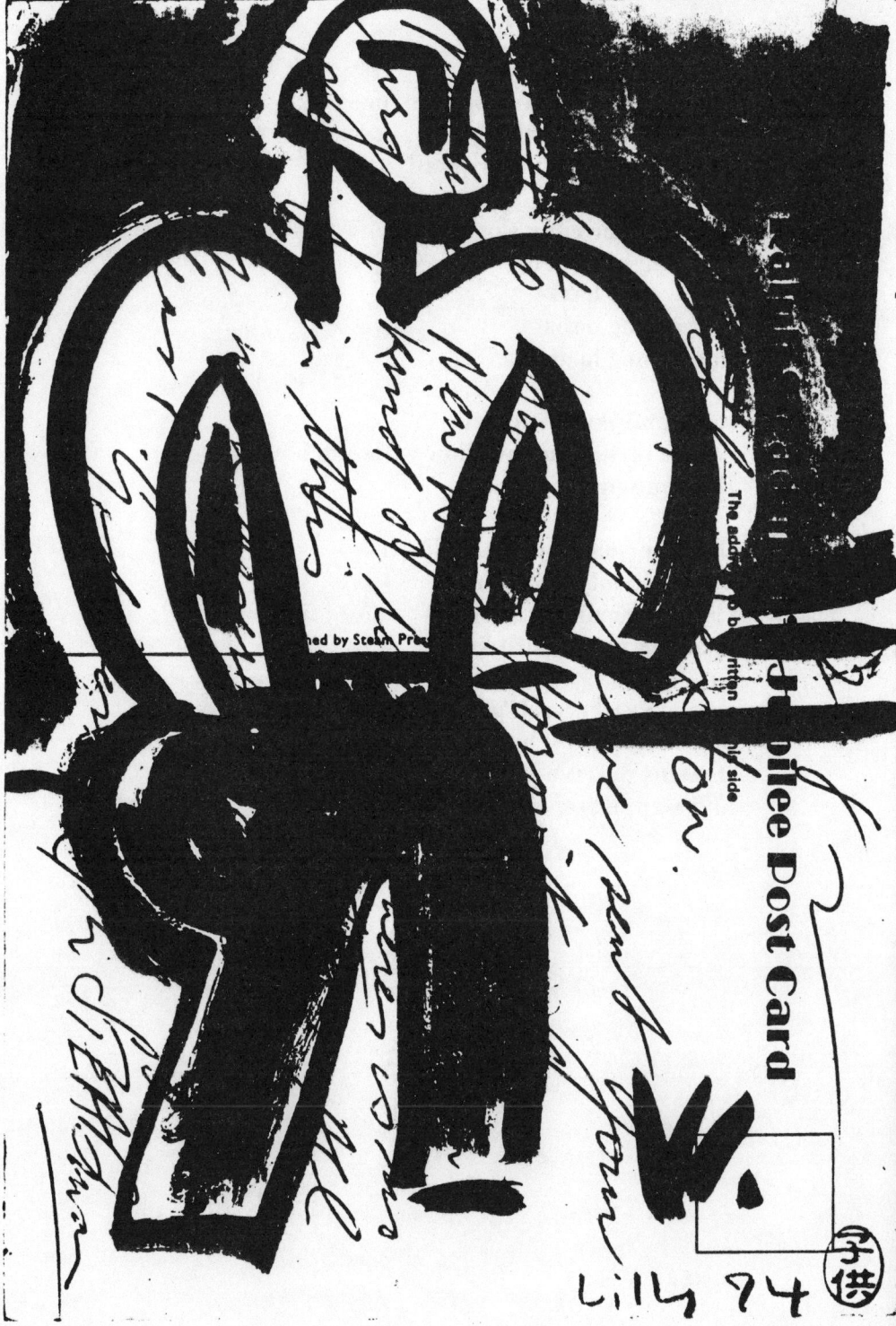

tears like jewels

it seems i went down
but not far enough
i thought i was in hell
but i was way too happy

whoring and boozing till 4 am
shit i didnt see day lite
for 15 winters

no im exagerating
i was a shit drunk
just as my poetry
is romanced to nothing

next time i go visiting
i vow never to water a drink
or refuse a smoke
ile wear stones in my boots
and shed tears like jewels

tha... you ... coutishly f... your gra...
Cuckoo Songs, Perh... ...is and other
anspe... ... organs.

Keep ... ing that wild & ... p...
where ... Muse leadeth ... istell...

Count Min..., I have seen ...nce ...nce
return to ...se from An... ...heo...

fear ...ot. The Poe... wil... ...
destroyed ...ough hordes ... ...nind... ...
destroyed ...ems.

...urab... ...rade... Aye,

Richardos Bumofski

lily 84

either all are special
or none are special

i walk in a holy manner

i paint in a holy manner

i rite in a holy manner

either all are special

or none are special

i walk in a holy manner

GUILDFORD
15 APR
1988
SURREY

Billy Childish
Poet and
Painter.
2 May Road.
Rochester. KENT.

billy

billy gets drunk
billy does yoga
billy climbs a mountain
billy goes canoeing
billy werks in the dockyard
billy goes whoring
billy leaves school
billy falls in love
billy rites a book
billy makes a record
billy paints a thousand pictures
billy draws all summer
billy meditates
billy hurts his knee
billy tattooes his body and travels to japan
billy looks for god in all the rong places
billy laughs
billy remembers how to cry
billy becomes bitter
billy smiles
billy makes a gun
billy is hungry
billy is found wanting
billy learns to celebrate
billy learns to forgive
billy fights with his father
billy stubs a cigarette out on his own hand
billy punches a wall
billy nearly drowns in a swimming pool
billy changes his name twice in the same week
billy changes everything
billy shoots an arrow
billy becomes angry
billy cooks with a skillet
billy eats fruit
billy builds a fire

this is all

as you can imagine
the people are hartly sick
of hearing of all the achievements
of this person

97

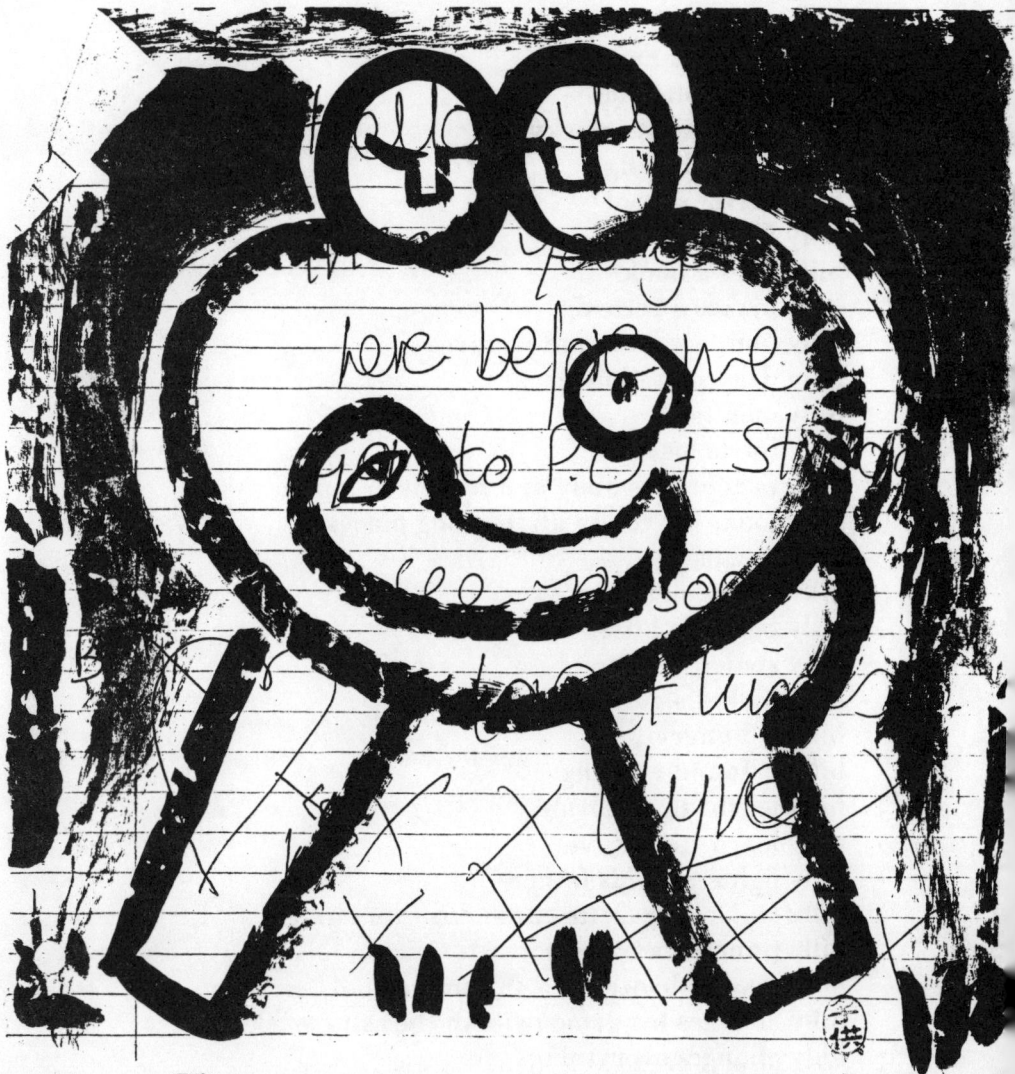

6.94

in five minites
youll know me

how will you know me?
these poems with no teller
given in love
ten bright badges of hell

poems for dear whores who
im loathed to fuck
poems for the lost
for the smiling of hell
poems for thieves in fear
and wives in grief

poems that sapped my father
poems for brave harts
not for my brother
but for the brothers
not for my mother
but for the mothers

poems proven as curses
poems plain as flowers
poems as bible
open and closed

A legendary figure in underground writing,
painting and music, Billy Childish was born
in Chatham, England in 1959. He has
published over 30 collections of his poetry
and featured on over 70 independent LP
records. His poems have been translated into
several languages and he has exhibited his
paintings in London, Hamburg and Paris.
He continues to write and paint in Chatham.

Other Titles available in Hangman Books

Companions in a Death Boat	B. Childish
The English Scene	V. Templar
6 Turkish Tales	T.K. Emin
Communion	B. Lewis
The Man who Created Himself	S. Ming
One Clever Kid	J. Corkwell
Cannon-Fodder	L.F. Céline
51st Anniversary	V. Templar
Fish Glue in Eskimo Land	S. Ming
Feverish Musk	S. Ming
Sermons	S. Ming
King of the Crypt	J. Corkwell
Lonely Hearts and Casualties	C. Broderick
Rumba Rumba	N. Sparkes
Childs Death Letter	B. Childish
May my Piss be Gentle	M. Lowe
Creosote Kingdom	V. Templar
Like a God i love all Things	B. Childish
The Hart Rises	B. Childish
120 Pigs and Me	M. Lowe
Self-hate in a phone-free Heaven	D. Belton
Here Endeth the Parish of Chatham	C. Broderick
Trembling of Life	B. Childish
Poems of Laughter and Violence	B. Childish
Days with a Hart like a Dog	B. Childish
Poems to Break the Harts of Impossible Princesses	B. Childish

Available from:
Compendium Books, Camden.
Dillons, Long Acre.
Hatchards and other good bookshops.

BLACK HAND DISTRIBUTION
2 May Road
Rochester
Kent ME1 2HY

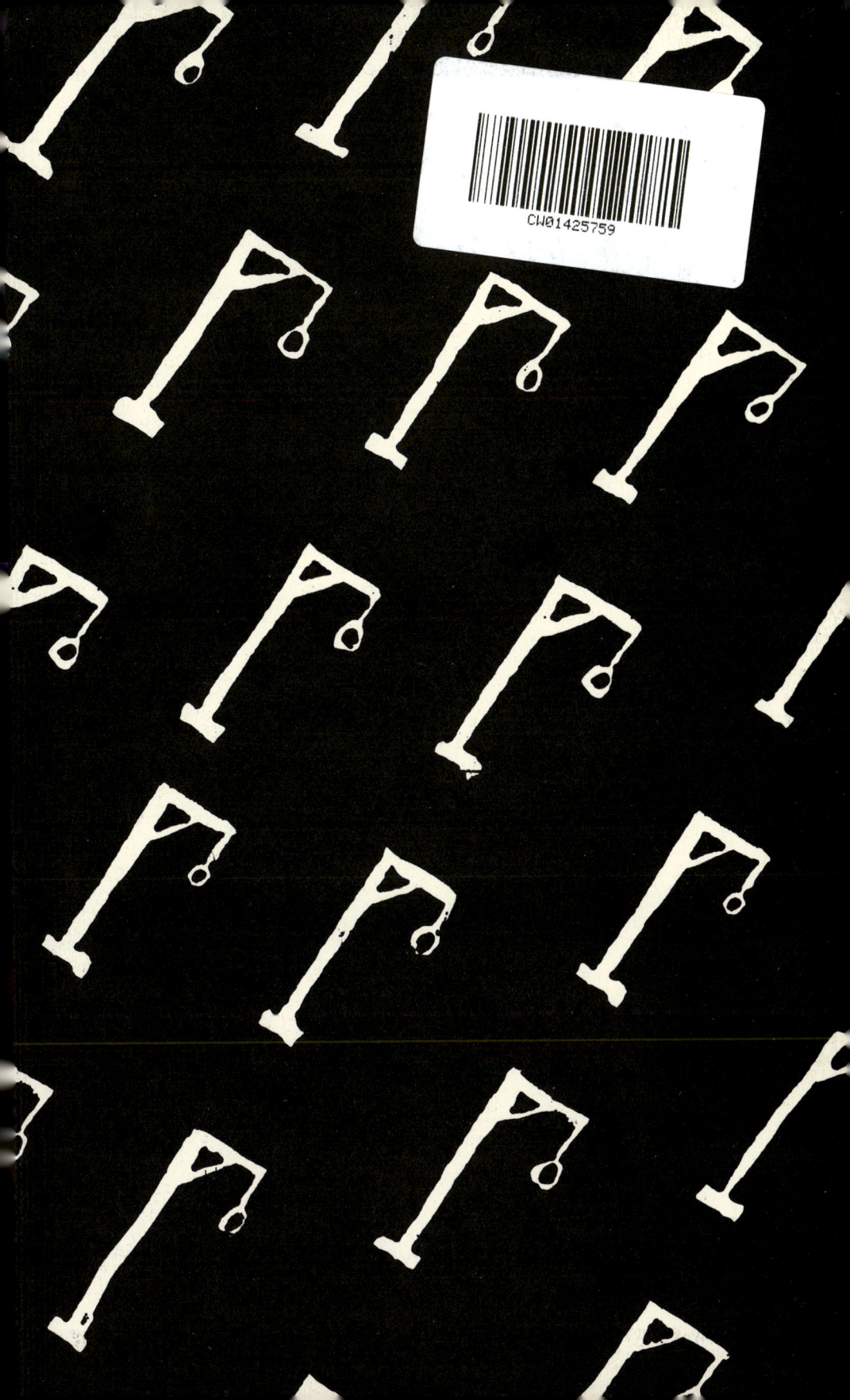